Costume Reference 10

1950 to the Present Day

MARION SICHEL

B.T. Batsford London

First published 1979
© Marion Sichel 1979

ISBN 0 7134 1509 6

Printed in Great Britain by
The Anchor Press Ltd.
Tiptree, Essex
for the Publishers B.T. Batsford Ltd,
4 Fitzhardinge Street, London W1H 0AH

Contents

5   Introduction

9   Men
25   Women
63   Children

65   Glossary
69   Select Bibliography
71   Index

Introduction

The appearance of a new fashion does not necessarily mean a total change of style; it may be only a matter of details such as trimmings and accessories. With greater and swifter communications, due to films and television as well as magazines, fashions not only changed more often but also spread faster than ever during this period.

Many fashions were in fact fashions of the past being revived, and usually altered a little. This recycling (fashions go in thirty year cycles) was greatly influenced by modern developments, not only scientific and marketing advances but by social trends, for instance the independence and equality of women.

New production methods and synthetic materials not only replaced, they added to the natural materials. The introduction of quick-drying non-iron fabrics made it possible to have delicate and light coloured garments for everyday wear, even in grubby cities.

The new methods of mass production did much to lower prices and bring fashion to the masses, and the increasing number of women going out to work meant that they had that much more to spend on clothes anyway.

This period, in fact, probably saw more of a revolution in fashion than any other. The general levelling-off in society (as well as the points mentioned above) meant that fashion could originate on the street rather than filter down from the top as it had always done in the past. This gave us such popular trends as Teddy Boys, blue jeans, punk and so on.

The other great change of the period was that of the 'age' of fashion. Previously fashion had been designed with the mature man and woman in mind. Now, in the explosion of British designers that made up the 'swinging sixties' and took over the lead from France and Italy, fashion was designed specifically for the young and adapted/adopted afterwards by their elders. Mary Quant invented the mini skirt and hot pants and in Carnaby Street John Stephen designed for the young men.

Boutiques (these had originated in Italy) sprung up everywhere in England to sell the new colourful and original clothes to the young and trendy and stores opened special departments for them. Mary Quant set up a wholesale business, the Ginger Group, in 1963, to produce her own clothes — gymslip dresses, short skirts, casual coats and striped tights.

This revolution hastened the decline of haute couture which was already feeling the ill effects of the post-war growth in mass-produced clothes which were not only cheap but of a higher quality than previously. One of the few French couturiers of any real importance to survive the modern trends was Yves St Laurent. About 1971 he gave up his fashion house and turned to designing for the ready-to-wear market. Courregès was another couturier who went into this market when he designed flat, usually white boots which became 'the thing' to wear with mini skirts, and Pierre Cardin brought in Space Age fashions. These dress designers, as well as others such as Hardy Amies, rather than the old bespoke tailors of Savile Row, began to design men's wear.

Many of the famous designers, in order to remain prominent, gave their names to commercial enterprises as well as to off-the-peg clothes, for instance towels, ties, soap, perfumes, chocolates.

Clothes were generally worn for ease, comfort, convenience and practicability and were fairly simple. Women's dresses became shorter with the mini and hot pants then longer with the midi and maxi. Trouser suits evolved as a contrast and have remained a lasting favourite.

By the 1960s formal and casual clothing had merged. The same type of clothes were worn for day as for dinner wear; dresses might be worn long or short, neither looking out of place on most occasions.

In the 1970s fashions became freer, without set clothes for any but the most formal occasions. Tweedy, ethnic, glamorous, nostalgic, classic or pretty clothes could be worn at all times.

1972 brought more emphasis on width with tent coats,

beltless chemise dresses, kaftans, etc., all being very popular. Ethnic costumes were also used as the basis for fashion ideas, for example the Bavarian dirndl, the French Basque beret, Chinese jackets with their mandarin collars and Japanese kimonos.

In the late 1970s classic styles, clothes such as twin sets and feminine dresses began to replace the almost fashion-less clothes that had prevailed until then.

As soon as clothes rationing ceased the cut of men's suits became exaggerated. High buttoned coats and tight fitting trousers, resembling the Edwardian styles, became the mode. They were generally worn with winkle picker type shoes. At the same time another fashion appeared, the Zoot suit. Worn mainly by the Teddy Boys, this was influenced by the tough guy image of certain film stars. These suits had long jackets with velvet collars and were worn with thick crêpe-soled shoes or boots.

In the late 1960s fashions took on a clearly militaristic look — epaulettes on sports coat shoulders, the trench coat and British warm were all the fashion, as well as student's peaked caps and chevrons sewn on to sports shirts as decoration.

Men's fashions evolved from the Edwardian revival and longer hair styles to printed and striped shirts worn without ties and polo neck jumpers. Hardy Amies, apart from designing clothes for women — mainly sensible ready-to-wear suits, coats and dresses — also designed men's clothes for mass production. He developed the typical man's outfit of the 1960s which included shirts, ties, sports jackets and short motoring coats as well as knitwear and men's shoes. During this period men generally became far more fashion conscious.

The width of men's shoulders became broader with the use of padding and jackets became looser fitting while trousers widened. The whole posture became more relaxed. The new casual trend manifested itself in the replacing of waistcoats by jerseys. The width of men's trousers fluctuated as much as the length of women's skirts. Gradually, many unessential but traditional items of clothing were discarded: hats were on the way out as well as ties. Teenagers wore leisure shirts in the 1960s without ties but with pinned or tabbed collars.

Waistcoats also went into decline as the trend for hipline trousers, or hipsters, emerged. For a brief while in the late 1960s waistcoats were worn formally but this fashion did not last as the trend towards greater ease and comfort was permitted by modern materials and techniques which, however, allowed smartness to be retained.

The world-wide fashion of blue jeans in the 1970s began in the 1850s when Levi Strauss originally made them in canvas. Later on they were made in twill or denim with the seams reinforced with copper rivets. They are probably the most universal item of clothing worn by both rich and poor alike, women as well as men, from as early as the 1930s.

Make-up acquired greater prominence as outward appearances became more important. After-shave lotions and deodorants also became common.

Cloche type hat. The dress, with a shirtwaister top, has a gored skirt. The corduroy blazer is edged in a colour to match the dress, c. 1974

Men

Single-breasted leisure jacket in hopsack. The hairstyle is still short and brushed back, c. 1963

Lounge suits were normal wear throughout the period for both informal evening wear and daytime attire. Lounge coats and sports jackets often had side vents or central back vents. Suits were quite conventional until the early 1960s when single-breasted styles had three to four buttons, instead of the usual two. Jackets became more fitted and waisted as well as slightly longer. In the mid-1960s jackets tended to have lower waists and they were more flared with longer side vents. Pockets with flaps tended to be set at more of a slant and the sleeves flared at the cuffs. By the mid-1960s double-breasted jackets sometimes fastened fairly high with six buttons and the pockets were also slightly slanting.

In the mid-1950s an Italian-inspired fashion became popular. The suit jacket was so short that the back often rode up; it was also made to fit very tightly. The trousers were made on the skimpy side and slightly short. These suits were worn with shoes that had pointed toes and the whole effect was of a tightness and squatness that was not at all elegant. This fashion did nevertheless remain fairly popular for around eight years.

As a suit is expensive and represents a substantial investment, the most versatile colours and designs tended to be worn. The conservativeness of design of the average .suit extended to the fashionable suit which varied very little throughout the period. In fact the basic design has remained much the same apart from minor details such as the width of shoulders and lapels and the placing of buttons; the width of trouser legs also varied from time to time.

The couple on the left are wearing unisex clothes, c. 1969, and the girl on the right is in a shirtwaister and casual shoes

The tweed leisure jacket is low cut with flapped pockets. The tie is broader than in the 1960s. The hair is blow-dried to give it more body, c. 1978

From the early 1950s many suits were made of man-made and 'wash-and-wear' fabrics that needed little or no ironing. The trend was also towards lighter weights, as improved home heating and better transport lessened the need for heavier and warmer materials.

Jackets and coats became slightly broader across the shoulders, more shaped to the waist and then slightly flared around 1967. Trousers and slacks also became more tapered. Mix and match clothing became fashionable from the 1960s.

In the late 1960s men's clothes altered a little. Jackets were cut higher and flared from the waist, and trousers also became flared from the knees. Even the more conservative suits and jackets followed these lines. In 1968 the typical city gentleman wore a bowler hat with a curled brim, a fob watch, a neatly furled umbrella, a silk tie and in his left breast pocket a handkerchief folded so that two points showed.

In the 1970s, although suits remained basically the same, wider lapels, broader shoulders and more shaping at the waistline became popular. Trousers also tended to vary slightly and were sometimes flared from the knee.

From the middle of the 1970s suits, which had gone out of fashion except for business and formal occasions, became popular again and were very often three piece: jacket, trousers and waistcoat. The shoulders were fairly broad as were the collars but the jacket remained waisted. High collars on jackets were also fashionable but these gradually became lower again. Occasionally waistcoats had small roll collars.

SHIRTS

From the 1950s men's shirts were made in a greater and bolder variety of colours than previously. Checks or stripes and a great range of patterns was available. Dark shirts were often worn with light coloured ties which also came in various designs ranging from paisley patterns to spots and stripes. Knitted ties were worn as well.

From about 1953 shirts were made in non-iron man-made materials blended with cotton. They were often cut straight at the base instead of having the usual tails so that they could be worn casually outside trousers or shorts. Jacket styles were popular and sleeves could be long or short.

Styles became increasingly diverse, shirts being made with anything from polo necks to frilled fronts or jabots for formal wear, while for everyday wear or casual occasions floral prints were worn. Indian style shirts, often in cheese-cloth, and bright colours became the mode. Towards the end of the 1960s it became popular for evening shirts to be of striped materials.

In the early 1970s when knitted materials became so fashionable that almost any article of clothing could be made up in some type of knitted fabric, casual shirts were also made in a variety of cottons, wools or man-made fibres. The fronts might be zipped or fastened with buttons or even cross lacing.

In the 1970s shirts were made fitted to the waist to give a slimmer silhouette. The pointed collars that had been so popular in the 1960s gradually became shorter.

T-shirts, popular from the early 1970s, were often decor-ated on the front with names, advertisements or cartoon characters; in fact from the mid-1970s almost anything might be printed on them.

NECKWEAR

Ties became wide and scarves were also worn much more for casual occasions. The scarves were generally nylon, silk or cotton and either tied in the front or held together with an ornamental ring.

From the middle of the 1970s ties were often omitted or replaced by neckerchiefs and the shirt collar left open. Shirt collars could also be worn over the jacket collars.

TROUSERS

From the early 1950s to the early 1960s there were some-times turn-ups on trousers after which date they were gener-ally omitted. Trousers were cut more tapered to the ankles and were often, when informal wear was required, of a darker shade than the jacket worn with them. For country wear trousers and jackets were worn in matching tweed. Corduroy trousers were also popular from the 1950s onwards.

From the mid-1950s trousers were made more shapely with a waistband that had elastic inserted; this could be used to tighten the waistline by buttoning so that pleats were no longer required. Zip fronts became usual. The crease down the fronts of the trouser legs was permanently pressed.

Men's trousers gradually became tighter fitting, this trend beginning in the late 1940s with the advent of the Edwardian Look and continuing right into the 1960s when they became

Single-breasted suit with low lapels, c. 1965

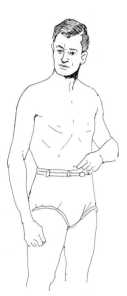

Swim briefs, c. 1967

Underwear — briefs and vest. The vests were later worn as ordinary tops, c. 1968

so narrow that they had to be made shaped instead of straight as the wider trousers had been.

By 1965 there was a fashion for tucking the trouser bottoms into the top of calf length boots which were specially designed for that purpose.

Cross pockets on trousers were more popular than the normal pockets down the side seam as they were easier to get at with the tighter trousers, especially when sitting in the new lower cars.

Trousers that flared slightly from the knees became fashionable about 1966 and hipster trousers that fitted just over the hips became popular at about the same time. By around 1972 the hipster trousers were fuller although bell bottoms, which had been fashionable a few years previously, remained in vogue.

SPORTS AND INFORMAL WEAR

There was a tendency towards greater informality and towards the wearing of less conventional clothing for sports. Open-necked shirts, trousers or slacks worn with sports jackets were generally worn by men for many sporting occasions while women preferred skirts and blouses or trouser suits as well as pinafore dresses to more formal wear.

Tennis outfits for men hardly altered from the previous period. White shirts and shorts perhaps with a V-necked pullover were popular, worn with white socks and laced rubber-soled canvas shoes. Tennis trousers were discarded for the more practical shorts and the only sport that now retained trousers was cricket.

In 1963 the first beach hats incorporated a zipped compartment in the crown to hold all the odds and ends that are usually carried in a pocket. For beachwear mini pants or jeans cut as brief as possible were popular in the 1970s. They were very often worn without any top or with old-fashioned sleeveless undervests which were available in a variety of colours. Casual shirts were also worn, often left unbuttoned. Bathing costumes were worn very brief.

Football shorts also became as brief as possible and the shirts were made of lightweight materials. Football boots, now more like heavy shoes, became the mode.

For leisure wear bush jacket styles were worn both in and out of doors, replacing shirts and jackets. Hip length overcoats were worn if the weather was cold. Battledress blouse designs were adopted for informal wear as were the sleeveless leather coats and padded jackets of the R.A.F. These proved especially popular for motor cyclists and were the forerunners of anoraks.

For summer wear many casual jackets were made unlined. Corduroy jackets and gabardine jackets that could be zipped up the front were also popular. By the end of the 1950s cardigan jackets without collars or lapels often replaced tweed jackets for casual wear; they were made in a variety of materials such as plain cloths or jersey knits. By the 1960s sweater jackets with raglan or set-in sleeves and small collars were also worn. Many of these cardigan type jackets had leather or suede front panels. There was an increasing variety of cardigans and pullovers, either fairly lightweight or made up in chunky wools. V necks were popular as were crew and polo necked styles. From the mid-1960s Arran style sweaters as well as striped jumpers became the mode.

From the end of the 1960s safari-style casual suits became fashionable. Denim suits and separates were also worn, but mainly by the younger generation who also wore hipster jeans and T-shirts.

Knitted materials became very fashionable, fitting in with the ever popular casual look. Anything from suits and shirts to ties might be made up in one of the many knitted fabrics.

Single-breasted jackets became more popular than the double-breasted styles. Separate jackets and slacks were increasingly worn, even for business wear, thus allowing for a more flexible 'mix and match' approach. The casual look spread from the purely informal situation right up to board-room level. By the mid-1970s leisure suits were two piece outfits consisting of slacks and short jackets. The jackets were generally fairly high lapelled with patch pockets and were either belted, half belted or tied around the waist. Turtle necked sweaters, casual shirts or T-shirts might be worn with these suits. Ties and scarves were optional.

Jeans, popular throughout the period, were often worn with high boots and open necked shirts beneath which, in the mid-1970s, a vest might be seen. T-shirts with all kinds of imprint also remained popular.

The 'layered' look, the wearing of one item of clothing over another became fashionable in the mid-1970s. Short sleeved vests or T-shirts were worn over long sleeved shirts, sweaters could be worn one over the other and loose casual jackets worn over anything. Edwardian clothing became popular from the end of the 1940s. The Neo-Edwardians, or Ivy League as they were also known, expressed a nostalgia

Double-breasted blazer with flapped pockets. The casual shirt is worn without a tie, c. 1972

Casual jacket with a zip fastening and patch pocket. The cuffs and waistband are of a knitted material. The trousers, without turn-ups, had cross pockets and a buckled belt. The top is a polo necked sweater, c. 1968

Rock-and-rollers of 1956. The boy is in a typical Teddy Boy outfit and the girl is wearing a very full dirndl-type skirt and plain V necked top. Her hair is tied back in a pony tail

for past elegance which was reflected in their clothes, the style of which was created by West End tailors. The jackets were tight fitting, buttoning high at the neck, and had long skirts with either one or two vents at the back. They often had velvet faced collars and cuffs. The waistcoats were embroidered or of brocade and could have stepped collars. The trousers were made very narrow fitting. Such an outfit might be worn with a small bowler hat, and pointed toe shoes, 'winkle pickers'.

Teddy Boy styles, also Edwardian in outlook, were not intended as a nostalgic reminiscence but rather as a break-away from traditionalism and were worn by the less elegant. The Teddy Boy look was popular in the 1950s among teen-agers who wanted to look tough although the 'Teds' of 1956 inclined more to nostalgia for the elegance of past fashions. Their dress consisted of a longish jacket almost reaching the knees; this was single-breasted with wide padded shoulders known as 'drapes'. Embroidered waistcoats and drainpipe trousers or jeans which were almost skin tight were also worn and very narrow 'bootlace' ties. The shoes usually had thick crêpe soles but might be winkle pickers.

Hairstyles were fairly long and greasy looking with a quiff in the front while the sides were brushed towards the centre back. Sideburns reaching the base of the ears were popular. This entire style of fashion was again popular for a brief while about 1977-78.

Another 1950s phenomenon were the 'beatniks' who went in for colourful open-necked shirts and corduroy trousers. Velvet suits with trousers tight to the knees and then flared out were considered elegant. Suits were made in a variety of bright colours in contrast to the standard greys, browns and black.

After the late 1950s Teddy Boy styles became less fashion-able. Trousers with turn-ups became usual and a more clean-cut look was popular — well polished shoes, short hair, etc. About 1962 the Beatles, a teenage pop group, had a great influence on clothing and hairstyles. They popularised longer hair worn brushed forward and also more colourful clothes.

The Mods and Rockers in the mid-1960s both simulated the Teddy Boy image in different ways. The Mods adopted Italian type hairstyles and jackets, suede chukka boots or crêpe-soled shoes and shaped trousers. The rockers wore their hair long and had leather jackets with metal stud decorations, boots that zipped up and drainpipe jeans. Hell's Angels were dressed similarly.

The girl is dressed in a mini — Twiggy style with very short hair, c.1966. The boy in the centre has a Beatle hairstyle and wears a collarless jacket and tight trousers, also of the Beatle era, c. 1962. The man on the right is in a single-breasted suit, c. 1969

Another 'tough guy' image that sprang up among teenagers in the early 1970s was that of the skinheads, youths with their hair almost shaven off, wearing trousers with the bottoms rolled up and with coloured braces. Shirts were always either checked or in gingham. 'Bovver' boots (thick heavy boots) were also indispensable.

Another set of youngsters who had a profound effect on young fashion were the 'Flower People' or hippies, of the late 1960s. They originated in California, USA, and the style of their clothes was largely inspired by the USA.

The Carnaby Street image which originated in England was influenced by all these styles but developed its own elegant modern mode which was available through the new men's boutiques.

EVENING WEAR

About 1953, when for very formal occasions tailcoats were worn, the tails were square cut. From the mid-1950s the tails became narrower and slightly longer, the lapels also becoming more narrow. However, tailcoats were not much worn, except by waiters, and towards the end of the period were only worn on the dance floor for competition dancing.

From the beginning of the 1960s morning coats were worn with grey or check trousers; the entire suit might occasionally be of a grey material.

Dinner jackets were generally single-breasted although in the 1950s double-breasted ones were also worn. The lapels were usually faced with silk. Towards the end of the 1950s shawl collars became fashionable, becoming narrower in the 1960s; these were generally of ribbed silk. Wide cummerbunds were also modish.

By the mid-1960s many evening suits were similar in cut to day lounge suits, but were made without ticket pockets and without flaps to the breast pocket. Dinner jackets remained in fashion in dark blue and black, the members of dance bands often wearing them in various other colours until the later 1950s. Formal evening wear became generally less usual during the period. Theatrical occasions for instance no longer called for evening dress apart from gala occasions and when Royalty was present.

Men became more fashion conscious than previously in the 1960s and evening shirts were made more ornate than those worn for the daytime. The fronts were often tucked or could be of frilled lace, the cuffs being made to match

Beret with a small peak, and a blazer type casual jacket, c. 1976

*Shortish raincoat with a fly
fronted fastening, c. 1972*

by the mid-1960s. Frilled fronts might be bought separate and buttoned on to a plain day shirt. For a very short while in the early 1960s evening shirts had roll necked collars. In the 1970s many shirt fronts were of broderie anglaise. Black ties or bow ties of silk or velvet were usually worn with evening attire.

OUTDOOR WEAR

Coats varied very little, being fairly long and full with collars and revers; they were often belted, especially raincoats. As the 1950s progressed, shorter above-the-knee overcoats became more popular, especially for wearing in cars. Many were made in sheepskin or suede and were mainly single-breasted. These short coats seldom had belts.

Overcoats, both single- and double-breasted, differed little from those of previous periods. They could have either set-in sleeves or be of the raglan type. The city gent's coat, instead of being the more usual above-the-knee length, was worn slightly longer and often had a velvet faced collar. Coats were often made in less heavy materials than previously, sometimes of a shower-proofed gabardine. Many coats were made to accommodate a detachable zipped-in warm lining.

In the early 1960s car coats, which were shorter than ordinary overcoats, were worn by most men. Tall firm hats were also found to be impractical in cars so if any headwear was worn at all, soft felt hats or caps were chosen. Light-weight suits were also found to be more practical with the greater use of cars; heavyweight materials were used less and less, becoming unfashionable. Overcoats continued to get shorter: by 1966 they were so far above the knee that they resembled jackets, except that they were usually of a heavier material. Just as winter coats and jackets were in a similar style, so for summer wear were shirts and casual jackets.

From the late 1960s overcoats, when worn, were more flamboyant, becoming longer waisted and slightly flared with large collars and lapels. Leather and fur as an access-ory on collars and cuffs became fashionable and the materials generally became less and less bulky and heavy. Coats became almost maxi in length and could be tied around the waist with a belt instead of being buckled. Other coats were quite short, ending just above the knees; these were very practical as car coats. Large patch pockets became modish in the late 1970s.

Shoe styles varied little, but the overall variety became greater. Chelsea boots and slip-ons, rather than laced shoes, were popular for everyday wear. Men also wore sandals and sports shoes in summer for informal occasions.

Suede shoes were popular for casual wear, as were sandals and slip-ons which very often had a small elastic strip under the leather in the front or at the sides to facilitate putting them on. Teddy Boys wore heavy shoes with thick crêpe soles. Towards the end of the 1950s Italian style shoes became the mode. These were lightweight and well fitted. Stainproof and water-repellent leathers also came on to the market at this time.

High boots with slightly higher heels than usual were worn from the early 1960s. These were popular with the narrower tapered trousers. Extremely pointed toes, similar to women's winkle pickers, were also popular amongst men, especially for town wear. From the mid-1960s ankle boots with flattish heels and crêpe soles were as popular as canvas shoes for casual wear.

In the mid-1960s boots for men, reaching the ankles, became very popular; there were many designs, the Chelsea boot being one of them. The sides had an elastic gore to give them a better fit, as often there was no means of fastening.

By the late 1960s shoes tended to be more of the moccasin style for casual wear and elasticated Chelsea boots and laced shoes were seen less. Also in the late 1960s shoes were round and square toed but less bulky in look than previously. Then in the early 1970s they became higher heeled with the heels reaching from 5 to 10 cm and the rounded toes became slightly curved up. Boots were also being worn on casual occasions from the 1970s.

Running shoes and various types of plimsolls or training shoes, also known as sneakers, became very popular in the 1970s, and Levis who had originated jeans began to make

Slip-on shoe with a buckle, mainly as ornamentation, c. 1969

Slip-on shoe with elasticated sides, c. 1970

Slip-on shoe, c. 1969

Slip-on with gusset under the front flap, c. 1963

Casual shoe with a pocket at the side and thick crêpe soles, c. 1977-1978

Chukka or casual Chelsea boot, c. 1972

Boot with eleasticated sides and a tag at the back, c. 1963

Slip-on shoe with chisel toe,
c. 1972

Slip-on, 1964

Trainer or running shoe for
casual wear, c. 1978

Ankle boots with a buckled
fastening, c. 1969

Laced shoe, c. 1972

canvas and leather type shoes to match their jeans. All these styles of shoes could be worn for casual wear.

In the mid-1970s white and black shoes, similar to the 'co-respondent' shoes of the 1930s again became fashionable.

From the 1960s men's socks, instead of being made of wool or cotton only, were made of nylon and man-made fibres or mixtures. Colours became more varied as did the designs, all sorts of stripes and patterns. Socks were also made shorter to end just above the ankles. The ribbing at the calf or ankle was of an elasticated yarn, thus making the socks self-supporting. From the mid-1970s, and mainly for winter wear, very thick and fluffy socks made in man-made fibres became popular.

HAIRSTYLES

The craze for 'rock and roll' from America created new styles for teenagers. Young men's hairstyles in particular became longer and the old 'short back and sides' was no longer fashionable. Although the long hair was not at first approved of by the older men (or indeed women), it was in fact only harking back to the past: long hair has been the fashion for more periods in history, the only times when short hair was popular being in the Middle Ages and in the 20th century when military wars dictated the more practical shorter hair.

After the second World War the Teddy Boys with their Edwardian styles moved towards longer hair. They wore their hair brushed up and forwards. One longer style, named after the film star Tony Curtis, had curly hair at the front. The D.A. was a variation of this style with the side hair brushed back to meet at the centre back, so that it had the look of a duck's tail. A style in complete contrast, the ultra-short crew cut, was also popular at this time however.

In the late 1950s and the early 1960s hair was still worn quite short but styled to give an illusion of length. Blow

Slip-on shoe

Casual shoe in leather or canvas,
c.1978

drying and waving techniques were employed to give the hair more body.

Both the beatniks of the 1950s and the hippies of the later 1960s wore their hair extremely long.

Longer hairstyles began to be popularised by pop singers in the early 1960s and although conventional hairstyles continued to be worn by older men the young, on the whole, increasingly went in for long hair, sometimes with a fringe and sideboards, a style popularised by the pop group, the Beatles. By the mid-1960s hairstyles tended not to have any parting, neither at the side nor in the centre.

Hairstyling as opposed to just having the hair cut became quite important for men at this time and hairstylists, as hairdressers became known, designed styles to suit individuals, although following the fashionable trends. Hair colouring and waving was also popular. It was at least partly due to improved cutting methods as well as to the use of hairsprays and setting or conditioning lotions that men increasingly wore their hair longer and in more flattering styles in the 1970s, even older men. By the late 1970s, however, almost any length was acceptable.

Hair pieces became very popular with men who were going bald and these could be designed in most styles. Hair weaving, another way to camouflage the fact that the hair is receding gave a very natural look. Planted hair could be treated almost as though it was part of the original hair.

Beards, moustaches and sideburns again became very popular in the 1960s. Sideburns might be long and straight or curly and wavy.

Soft leather hat

Cossack type hat in fur

Tyrolean style hat

Soft tweed hat, c. 1976

Beret type hat, c. 1976

Soft casual hat, c. 1976

HEADWEAR

Bowler hats were worn by city gentlemen. Trilbys were popular throughout the period. Many hats from the 1960s onwards were made of tweed or corduroy with tapered crowns and narrow brims. Tyrolean styles were also popular. In the extremely cold winter of 1964, fur Cossack-type hats became very fashionable. They could be made of sealskin, beaver or Persian lamb.

Men's hairstyles were still longish in the early 1970s and this meant that hats were not worn very much but as hairstyles became shorter again, about 1976, they regained popularity. They were made in a variety of styles from berets to hats with brims, mainly in materials that could be compressed without creasing so that the hat could be carried in a pocket if required.

BEAUTY AIDS

Men's toiletries, such as after-shave lotions, colognes, talcum powders and deodorants became very popular in the early 1950s; even socks were impregnated to make them smell sweeter!

From the mid-1960s instant sun-tanning lotions were as popular amongst men as amongst women. Hair sprays, lacquers and colour rinses were also beginning to be used by men.

ACCESSORIES

Neck chains and medallion belts became very popular in the late 1960s. Large buckled belts were also popular during this period.

Men began to use strapped shoulder bags which were

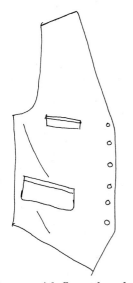

Waistcoat with slit pockets, c. 1963

Waistcoat with flapped pockets, c. 1963

Driving glove with perforated fingers

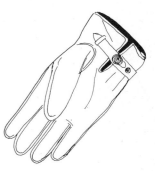

Glove with wrist fastening

extremely practical, allowing pockets to be emptied and thus giving a better line to clothes. Later these bags had just a small wrist strap.

In the late 1960s almost all shirt collars were attached to the shirt itself, thus making collar studs obsolete.

Scarves and gloves were also worn less because of the improvement in public transport, and also because many people had cars of their own; these meant that people walked less in the open.

Expanding metal armbands, which had been widely worn and were so important before shirt sleeves were made in varying lengths, were another commodity that ceased to be made.

Pyjama suits, night attire for men, were functional and made of opaque materials. Pyjama styles reverted to narrower trousers about 1959 when the fashionable lounge suit trousers narrowed.

Collapsible umbrella in a round case, c. 1963

Flat-cased collapsible umbrella, c. 1963

Furled umbrella with knotted cane handle

The girl in the large floppy hat is wearing a mini length 'space age' style dress with a very wide belt and a large buckle. The thigh length vinyl boots and extremely long gloves are fashionably shiny. The man on the right has a single-breasted long, lapelled jacket with the cuffs and collar faced in velvet. From the shoulders to the top of the pockets the ornamentation is also velvet. The shirt is frilled down the front and no tie is worn. The trousers are slightly flared from the knees and the shoes are of the slip-on variety.
The man on the left has a single-breasted casual jacket buttoning high up. Instead of a tie he wears a cravat. The trousers are straight with turn-ups.
The girl with the beret is wearing a 'skinny' polo-necked jumper. The casual trouser suit of shiny PVC is a unisex style. The jacket is high necked and fastens with press studs. The fairly tight trousers have a front zip fastening. A belt with an attached purse is worn, and a long, flowing scarf and large sunglasses complete the outfit. (Late 1960s)

The girl in the high stetson-type hat is wearing a mini two piece suit. The jacket is waistlength, double-breasted with short, deep lapels and large decorative buttons. The skirt is plain and straight. She is wearing wrist length gloves and seamless tights.

The girl sitting down has straight trousers that are worn over fairly high boots. The woolly buttoned-up cardigan has a scarf at the neckline and she is wearing a fashionable, thick plastic bangle on her wrist.

The girl on the right is wearing a twill summer trouser suit. The hip length jacket has short sleeves, and buttons up just off centre, being in a mandarin fashion. Around her neck she has a double-sided scarf. (Late 1960s)

Women

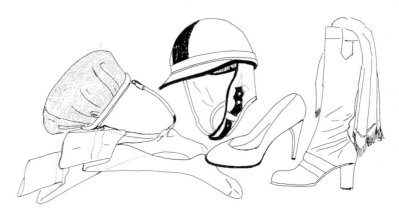

Dolman style suit with a straight skirt. The jacket has a flared basque. The hat is of the pillbox type, c. 1950

Sleeveless 'space age' dress, c. 1969

This was a time of extremes in women's dress, from minis (the shortest skirts in the history of fashion) to maxis, and from aggressive styles such as hot pants and Teddy Girl gear to the nostalgic and feminine floral prints of Laura Ashley. There were even topless clothes in 1964 when topless bikinis appeared on the scene.

Teddy Girls wore short fitted jackets over tight sweaters or jumpers and their skirts were generally very tight fitting and to mid-calf.

In the mid-1950s half belts on suits, coats and dresses, low at the back, were popular. (A feature of the coats and dresses of the 1970s was the trimming in real or imitation leather.) The A line launched by Christian Dior in 1955 lent itself well to classic suits. The jackets had fairly tight set-in sleeves, a very small collar and buttoned down the front. Checked tweeds were popular in this period. Generally the modern fashion was of a simple line and cut that suited most age groups and figures.

Loose weaves were popular for heavy materials and in 1963 the style of clothes had not altered much from the late 1950s with the full skirts, wide flared coats and small hats worn with accessories such as gloves, bags and shoes to match.

In 1969 the main fashion feature was the mini skirt, worn with tights, both designed by Mary Quant who also made the little girl look popular with gymslip dresses, shift and pinafore dresses. The mini·skirt (dresses were also made mini length) which dominated the 1960s and 1970s acceler-

On the left the girl is in a straight buttoned-through dress, sleeveless and with a round collar. A turban headdress and a long string of beads complete the ensemble, c. 1956. The other two girls are in minis, the centre one in a two-piece and a tall masculine hat and court shoes while the girl on the right is wearing high boots, c. 1969

ated the trend towards more sports type clothes and the move away from more formal modes of attire.

Skin tight sweaters that emphasised the figure and very brief bodices that revealed the midriff or see-through bodices were all worn with minis. The see-through bodice might be made of a semi-transparent material or of plastic link chains. Many mini dresses had a low décolletage or just had shoulder straps. The tights that were so essential a part of mini outfits were sometimes made of lurex or metallic thread as well as the cheaper nylon.

Mini styles caused underwear to be further abbreviated to the smallest of briefs and brassières. A very skinny look became desirable; this was exemplified by Twiggy, the most famous model of the era.

At the same time as the mini was popular, trouser suits became fashionable and richly embroidered and decorated ones became acceptable for evening wear. By the 1970s trousers were seen on women of all ages in all kinds of materials and styles.

Maxi, or ankle length, clothes, which had been abandoned after the First World War, suddenly appeared again in the

The felt cloche hat is worn over long straight hair. The suede short-sleeved jacket is made in a patchwork design and is worn over a jersey shirt with a long matching skirt. High boots were fashionable with this type of outfit, c. 1970

Tailored trouser suit with high necked blouse and bow at the neckline, c.1965

Mini dress with pleated skirt and scarf worn around the neck. Knee socks were also popular, c. 1968

Woollen two-piece costume in a mini length worn with a halo type hat, c. 1968

late 1960s in reaction to the minis. They were worn in the daytime and were often teamed up with matching sleeveless jackets or boleros which could be worn over pullovers or blouses.

The midi skirt, calf-length, which was popular in 1971, was worn with sleeveless or low necked tops.

In the early 1970s hot pants, originated by Mary Quant, were popular for a brief period. They were really just very short shorts for everyday wear, often worn with thigh high boots, very tight tops (with or without sleeves and often with patch pockets on the bust to emphasise the figure). Cartridge belts were also worn.

In the early 1950s popular fabric designs consisted of spots, lines and any vague patterns while from the mid-1950s floral cotton prints were very fashionable. In the late 1950s cotton was blended with man-made fibres to make it uncrushable, thus creating a fashionable and practical material for summer dresses. Previously silks were more widely used.

Television, by showing old films, recaptured the nostalgia of the 1920s, '30s, '40s, '50s and '60s in the 1970s. Biba, a boutique that became big in the early 1970s, recaptured the atmosphere of the 1930s. Laura Ashley, another boutique, sold Edwardian type clothes with small floral print designs.

Wide-sleeved kimono style top with a pencil skirt and pillbox hat. The handbag is of the envelope kind, c. 1957

DAY DRESSES

Sheath or shift dresses were very popular in the early 1950s. Asymmetrical styles were also popular with the drapery towards one side, pleats and flares also tending to be one sided. Halter necklines were worn on both formal and informal wear as well as low off-the-shoulder styles. Small waists were fashionable, the hips being emphasised to accentuate the waist. This effect could be achieved with large pouched or flapped hip pockets which might be stiffened. Large buttons and bows were also an important decorative feature on dresses.

Summer dresses were sleeveless or had small cap sleeves. They often had matching boleros with short or three-quarter length sleeves. Sloping shoulder lines were popular and these were accentuated by raglan or dolman sleeves. The more feminine style of dress that began with the New Look in 1947 continued into the early 1950s. The wasp waist was still fasionable, although skirts became less full from the waist, and the fullness began from the hips with either pleating or gores.

Trapeze style dress-coat, c. 1958

Dresses and ensembles of the 1950s

Permanently pleated straight dresses of man-made materials became extremely fashionable. They were generally sleeveless and had boat shaped necklines. Many were made in a jersey type of material that did not require the hemline to be sewn so that when the fashion was for shorter skirts, from about 1960, it was quite easy to cut a short length from the bottom. These dresses, quite plain, were sometimes worn with a belt and were often decorated at the neckline with long strings of beads.

An Empire line was achieved with a wide plain waistband on both day and evening dresses, either long or short.

In 1951 Christian Dior based his designs on the Princess line. The New Look, also created by Dior, in 1947, was in fact an interpretation of the 1915 styles with short tight bodices or jackets which were basqued and worn over longish, very full skirts. The next real change in fashion came in 1953, when Cristobal Balenciaga, a Spaniard, created a new silhouette which was straight and simple. Basically a sack shape, it was adapted to the chemise and tunic line. Sack dresses that were completely straight from the neck down were generally worn without belts. Many were made in ribbed jersey materials and had rounded necklines. They were sometimes also known as sheath dresses and were not dissimilar to the styles of the mid-1920s.

Sack dress and pochette handbag. The hat is small crowned with a large brim, c. 1958

From about 1954 Dior devised new silhouettes based on letters of the alphabet, the H line, the A line, the Y line and the S line, each giving a specific emphasis, such as wide shoulders, wide hems or straight and narrow skirts. He also created an interest in fuller skirts and a shortened form of the crinoline became very popular with teenagers in the late 1950s. It was fashionable to wear waisted dresses and knee length skirts that billowed out with the aid of cheaply produced paper nylon petticoats which rustled.

The Dior H line, launched about seven years after the New Look in 1954, comprised a short-skirted tubular shape with a low waistline which gave a flat chested appearance reminiscent of the 1920s. The A line could be achieved with fairly plain straight dresses that had a slight flare out to the hemline. Pouched jackets were sometimes worn with them. By 1955 both the A and the Y lines (with full dolman type sleeves and a tapering skirt) were fashionable.

Around 1956 tunic dresses were first worn and in 1958 Yves St Laurent, Dior's protégé, launched the 'trapeze' line. He also made black tunic dresses and trousers fashion-

Linen suit with maxi ankle-length skirt. The matching hat has a veil over the face, c. 1970

Woollen dress with a plain bodice, striped skirt and matching tie scarf, c. 1973

Long bloused jacket worn over a tight straight skirt, after Cardin, c. 1958

able. The loose hanging chemise style was originated by Balenciaga in 1957 and consisted of a loose tunic top worn over long straight skirts. Later the style was adapted and the sack dress came into being. Sack dresses usually had three-quarter length rather than long sleeves and the entire dress was very plain and simple.

Shift dresses often had matching jackets and could have belts if required. The waistline was fairly high in the late 1950s.

In 1954 Gabrielle Chanel, who had run a fashion house before the War, returned to designing her ever-popular classic suits and cardigan jackets without collars worn with blouses that had large bows at the neck. Her black dresses were also continuously fashionable during this period.

A style that did not remain popular for more than two or three years was a dress with a bouffant skirt that was gathered on to a band at the hem to make a barrel shape.

Sleeveless dresses became fashionable from the early 1960s. The three-quarter length sleeves that were popular in 1959 were less so from the early 1960s when long or short sleeves were again in the mode, although the longer sleeves were often worn pushed up to give a three-quarter length effect. For summer wear cap sleeves became fashionable as well as short sleeves although sleeveless dresses and tops were beginning to be seen frequently.

Clothes that could be worn both during the day and for evening, became very popular; afternoon dresses were now rarely seen.

From 1957 buttoned-through dresses with full skirts became popular. The necklines, which had generally been square or rounded, followed more of a shirtwaister style. By 1959, however, these full-skirted shirtwaisters, which had become very popular with the older generation, had gone completely out of fashion and they did not regain popularity until about 1961. There was a fashion for collarless jackets in the 1960s.

Beltless chemise dresses became fashionable in the early 1970s and trouser suits were gradually replaced by dresses and two piece dresses or suits. Large tent-like dresses became popular in the late 1970s.

SEPARATES, CASUAL AND INFORMAL WEAR

Separates were very popular from the mid-1950s onwards for leisure wear. Typical of the mid-1950s were off-the-shoulder tops with skirts, shorts or three-quarter length trousers or jeans.

Shirtwaister dresses, buttoned all the way down the front or just to the waist and worn with a belt, were always popular, the length depending on the prevailing fashion. The sleeves, either long or short, could be set-in or of the raglan type. Shirt blouses were popular with very full gathered dirndl skirts that were puffed out with stiffened petticoat slips.

Jackets with basques that could be slightly stiffened so that they stood out were small at the waist and fastened fairly high up. The sleeves were mainly of the raglan type and combined with the sloping shoulder line created a pyramid shaped silhouette. In the 1950s the collars were generally fairly high, but for afternoon or evening wear off-the-shoulder styles with draped collars were very fashionable. Tops or sweaters were sometimes made of the same material as the tights with which they were worn to give the impression of a leotard.

Tabards were also worn from the mid-1960s. They were sleeveless hip-length tops, both the front and back being alike and tied together at the sides, and were often worn over high necked jumpers.

Suede or leather waistcoats and jerkins were also worn. Sometimes just the front was of leather or suede and the back of a knitted material.

Sweaters became very thick and bulky and were often in cable stitch patterns, Arran designs being very popular in the early to mid-1970s. The sweaters or cardigans became so long at one point that they could also be worn as coats; they were sometimes referred to as 'granny coats'.

In the mid-1970s T-shirts as well as having advertisements and cartoons printed on the front also bore off-beat graphics of the 1920s and 1930s. Large numbers and stripes were also popular.

Victorian camisole tops, the old-fashioned laced and beribboned undergarments of the 1840s, became very fashionable worn with long evening skirts in the mid-1970s. From the mid-1970s also, vests came in all shapes and sizes from the traditional sleeveless top to the side vented vest; these were worn not as undervests but as tops with skirts or trousers.

In the later 1970s hooded jumpers with vertical pockets either side that could meet in the centre became popular.

Coolie style hat. The suit has a high buttoned jacket with long scarf and a pencil slim skirt, c. 1955

Suede flying jacket style, trimmed with sheepskin. The tight trousers are tucked into high boots, c. 1971

A high-buttoned shirtwaister dress with a wide decorated belt is seen on the left, c. 1954. In the centre the man is in a toggle-fastened duffle coat, c. 1952, and the girl on the right is in a shirtwaister dress with three-quarter length sleeves, c. 1956

These could be made of wool, cotton or man-made materials.

Blouses and tops became very voluminous and were known as blouson styles. The base could be tied or elasticated just below the waistline.

Bermuda pants with turn-ups and sometimes dipped in the front were popular for summer wear and could be worn with bikini type tops.

Casual skirts, pleated, flared or straight, worn with knitted sweaters or with blouses remained constantly in fashion, the skirt lengths varying according to the dictates of fashion.

Dirndl skirts were very popular from the 1950s. They were made to stand out with the aid of several frilled petticoats. Pencil straight skirts were also worn at this time.

Until the middle 1950s skirts remained at about mid-calf, after which they rose slightly. In 1950 straight skirts were usual but they could have inverted pleats or godets from the knee. From about 1958 skirts became shorter but remained below knee level.

For summer, skirts were generally very full and stiffened underskirts and frilly petticoats were all fashionable. Often, more than one petticoat was worn beneath the bouffant skirts.

By about 1960 skirts again became narrower, sometimes with a pleat at the back to allow for easier movement. In the early 1960s permanent pleats and crease-resistant materials enabled more fully pleated skirts to become the mode; these were popular for both day and evening wear. This method also enabled knife pleating to remain in position without the pleats falling out or seating.

When the mini skirt, designed by Mary Quant, first became fashionable in the mid-1960s, it was just an extremely short skirt that revealed gaily patterned and coloured tights which could range from thick knitted designs to thinner nylon textures including lurex.

In the late 1960s skirts became a little longer, falling about 5 to 10 cm above the knees, and in the mid-1970s long skirts, known as maxi skirts, became popular. These reached the ground and could be for day as well as evening wear.

In the late 1950s culottes or divided skirts were worn and were very practical for most occasions. Culottes became fashionable again in the mid-1960s and yet again in 1978, the skirts being made in such a way that the division was hardly discernable, being pleated or gathered.

Flounced mini dress and bubble cut hairstyle, c. 1968

The hat is of felt with large crown and brim. The dress, of the culotte type, has a split skirt and suede belt. The beads are fashionably long, c. 1970

Striped mini skirt worn with a square necked sweater and a floppy beret, c. 1972

In the early part of the century when trousers were first worn by women, they were known as pyjamas although they had nothing to do with night attire. From about 1936 they were known as slacks, a name that has survived to this day.

Blue jeans, first worn in America have been popular since the early 1960s. With the advent of unisex, women's trousers, instead of being zipped or fastened at the side, had the opening in the front, like men's trousers, and often girls did in fact wear men's jeans.

The shape of trousers varied from tight and straight to bell bottomed, and later they became wide all the way down. From time to time turn-ups became fashionable for brief spells.

Trouser suits were first worn in the mid-1960s. They were very adaptable, being made in a variety of materials from tweeds for daywear to lurex jersey for the evening. The jackets could be tailored or casual in style. In the late 1960s, trouser suits, instead of being just trousers and a jacket, sometimes consisted of a tunic dress worn over the trousers.

Slacks with a shirt worn on the outside and a belt, c.1970

Mini skirt with long sleeved blouse and a sleeveless sweater or tank top worn over it. The shoes are of the clog type, c. 1972

The mini tunic type dress is worn over patterned tights, c. 1970

Unisex look with blouson shirt and knee-length tight trousers, c.1970

Ensembles could include trousers, jackets, skirts and tunic dresses as well as matching waistcoats which could be worn in any combination with either a blouse or a sweater, thus making a wardrobe more versatile.

Trousers and trouser suits were accepted more and more and some restaurants where they had been banned had to relent and allow the wearing of them. The trouser suits of the 1970s were more feminine looking than those of the 1960s. They might comprise knitted tunic tops with a belt around the waist, safari type shirts or Cossack style blouses over knitted or cloth trousers. T-shirts or long ribbed sweaters, belted at the waist, were also popular with trousers as were midi length trench coats, long cardigans or vests, ponchos and capes.

Layers of clothing began to be fashionable around 1969, for instance a long sleeved shirt would be worn under a short sleeved pullover or sweater or a sleeveless vest. Long sweater coats could be put on over everything and a matching knitted cap and muffler or scarf complete the outfit. In the 1970s layered clothing remained popular with even short sleeved dresses being worn over long sleeved blouses. By 1978 the layered look might consist of as many items as a pair of trousers or skirt, a top (a blouse or jumper or both), waistcoat, jacket, another over-waistcoat, a coat or cape and a shawl.

By 1970 dresses and skirts could be worn any length from mini to midi and maxi. Trousers were also general wear.

By 1978 dresses were really beginning to look more feminine. They were often waisted with matching boleros and had full skirts edged with broderie anglaise or lace at the hemline or worn with lace or broderie anglaise edged petticoats which were allowed to show below the skirt hem.

A gipsy look was fashionable — a large fringed shawl worn over an embroidered frilly blouse with a full skirt and sandals — although sweaters and short skirts as well as short clinging dresses were still worn. The clinging effect could be achieved by the use of silk jersey or crepes or knitted fabrics.

Faster and easier travelling throughout the world led to the introduction of many foreign and ethnic styles of clothing including the kaftan, worn by both men and women. Cheesecloth shirts were worn by both sexes; these originated from India. Oriental fashions became the vogue in the 1970s.

Mini-skirted crocheted dress with tights decorated with metallic chains, c. 1968

Tweed trouser suit with a jabot fronted blouse, c. 1968

Jersey trouser outfit with top reaching the hips, c. 1970

Beret, and suit in mini length with patch pockets, c. 1973

Chinese workers' blue cotton loose-fitting jackets with mandarin collars became very popular as well as long kimonos with Chinese motifs. These could be worn for lounging or as evening wear.

Natural fibres gained in popularity over the man-made ones from the early 1970s, thus making wool and cotton more fashionable again. However fur fabrics remained popular, mainly because of the price of real fur and also for ecological reasons. With this return to natural fibres pre-wrinkled cotton and pre-washed and faded denim became the vogue from the mid-1970s.

KNITWEAR

Throughout the period knitwear was made of a great variety of man-made as well as natural fibres such as wool, cashmere, cotton. Crew necks, V necks and polo necks were all popular. The cardigans or pullovers could be plain or patterned or of Fair Isle designs. They were sometimes made to match the material of the dress or ensemble with which they were worn.

Classic twin sets, part of nearly every woman's wardrobe, were made in all yarns, generally of a fine texture. They usually comprised a plain jumper with a rounded neck and either long or short sleeves and a matching cardigan that either buttoned to the neck which was also rounded or was of a low V shape, the sleeves could be set in or 'fashioned' in the raglan style. Chunky and double knit wools were more popular with teenagers and their jumpers were often hip length and worn over skirts or trousers. Many were made in unisex styles, being worn by both boys and girls.

SPORTS WEAR

Sport and leisure wear became more informal so there was little need for special clothes for most sports.

About 1950 there were various kinds of swimming costumes from brief one piece to two piece costumes, the briefest of which were known as bikinis. The tops of the bikinis could be halter necked or have straps which could be removed for sunbathing. Sometimes the tops were boned and therefore didn't need further support. Many bikinis had separate skirts and/or short sleeved tops that could be worn over them on the beach. Bikinis became so minute in 1975 that they were held together just by string ties over the hips.

Swimsuits could be made in similar styles with the midriff of a mesh or transparent material.

One piece strapless swimsuits were popular from the 1950s. The tops were shaped and held in place by boning and padding which also gave a better bustline. Playsuits were made in a similar fashion with brief skirts attached and were very popular at this time.

For beachwear there appeared a variety of play clothes: jeans, shorts and Bermudas (knee length shorts) were all popular and were worn with gay coloured or checked shirts as well as lacey blouses that could be worn off the shoulder or tied under the bosom leaving a bare midriff.

For tennis, the innovations were 'Gorgeous Gussies' and the A line tennis dress. In 1949 lace-trimmed frilly panties (which became known as Gorgeous Gussies) worn beneath extremely short tennis skirts or dresses were made fashionable by Gussie Moran. Then about 1955, when the A line was popular, Teddy Tinling, who had designed Gussie Moran's fitted tennis dress and lacey panties, adapted the style for tennis wear in general.

There was no longer any special wear for motoring, on the contrary the car influenced all fashion to suit travel by car. Clothes suitable for car wear flourished, for instance, trousers, short sheepskin coats, flat shoes and headscarves while unsuitable clothes, such as tall and decorative hats fell into decline.

Shorts and sheath-like striped top worn for beach wear, c. 1972

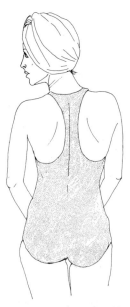

Low fronted swimsuit, c. 1970

Backless swimsuit, and headscarf tied behind the hair, c. 1974

Bikini swimwear, hair worn up in a 'beehive' style, c.1963

Swimsuit with a T back, and turban-like swim cap, c. 1974

Back view of tight fitting dress with halter neckline fastened with a bow at the back of the neck, c. 1973

Bouffant-skirted evening dress, gathered at the hem and trimmed with bows. Long evening gloves were worn and the hairstyle was short and curly, c. 1958

EVENING AND FORMAL WEAR

For weddings or cocktail parties it was usual to wear veiling embellished with velvet bows or flowers as headwear. Large artificial flowers worn in the hair sometimes replaced hats completely.

For afternoon and evening wear dresses had close fitting bodices and very full skirts that stood out with the aid of stiffened waist petticoats. These dresses usually reached about 15 to 20 cm from the ankles, just slightly longer than the day dresses. Ballet-length very full-skirted dresses in a flimsy material were very popular in the 1950s. They were often embroidered with sequins and stones and had a long flowing stole to match. The tops of the dresses were often of the halter neck style but could also have low décolletages or even be strapless, the bodice being boned to fit the figure.

Evening dresses in the early 1950s were often full and long or three-quarter length but by the 1960s long and full dresses were seldom seen. Short dresses became the mode except for balls and formal occasions when long evening gowns were still worn.

While the mini styles were in vogue, kaftans and long straight skirts were worn for the evening.

Velvet trouser suits were popular from the late 1960s and were worn with very ornamental and frilly blouses or ruffled jabots.

Dresses or skirts were very full with frilly tops or blouses. Shirt dresses in light and luxurious materials looked very elegant for evening wear.

A fashion that had been popular in the 1930s, the asymmetrical décolletage, one shoulder draped while the other was left bare, was again revived in the 1970s. There was also a revival of long skirts or dresses worn for semi-formal evening wear or for dinner parties. Almost any style could be worn in the late 1970s without it looking unduly dated.

Many dresses, blouses and jumpers were decorated with sequins and diamanté, either sewn on separately or appliquéed in ready-made designs.

Wedding dresses followed the fashionable lines and lengths of the period.

UNDERWEAR

After the War stockings were no longer considered an essential part of dress so suspender belts and corsets were less common. Cami-knickers and full length petticoats were also worn less. Underwear became more scanty: knickers became quite small, covering only the essential, and they became known as briefs. The main items of underwear worn were briefs, brassière, suspenders (if stockings were worn but even these became obsolete with the advent of tights) and slips, mainly from the waist.

Corsetry was revolutionised in the 1950s with the advent of elasticated yarn, which made it possible to have foundation garments without stiffening or whalebone that would still give firm figure control. Pantie girdles combined corset, suspender belt and knickers in one garment.

Girdles could still be worn as a combination with panties and were usually made of elasticated material. These supported the figure and had stocking suspender straps attached. Short girdles were mainly from the waist but longer ones reached well above the waistline and were often boned to accentuate the smallness of the waist; these were called waspies or corselets.

Bra-slips also came into fashion. These were brassières combined with slips. Materials for underwear became more lightweight and firmer, although still elasticated, Lycra being one of the first materials of that kind to be used.

Brassières were often padded or had bustforms of foam rubber inserted to give a fuller bustline. Inflated brassières were also on the market for a brief while but were not found to be very practical. Modern brassières are made to support the bust and achieve a particular type of bustline and of silhouette in general which is, for instance, very different from that which the Victorians aimed at. In the 1950s a pointed bosom was the ideal but in the 1960s, with the advent of the mini skirt, the emphasis moved to the legs and the bust and figure line became more natural looking. With Women's Liberation movements in 1970, around the 50th anniversary of Women's Suffrage, came the innovation of softer shaped brassières or the wearing of none at all.

Directoire knickers, which had been worn in the 1930s, but had given place to panties and briefs, were reintroduced in 1963. In the mid-1970s French knickers became the vogue. They had also been popular in the earlier part of the century and were loose-at-the-thigh and usually made of a silky material with lace insets or edging.

Stiff felt petticoats sometimes replaced the layers of petticoats worn beneath the full skirts of the 1950s. In the

Briefs and matching brassière, c. 1975

Knitted or crocheted woollen cap. The coat is mini length of the wrap-over style with a tied belt and beneath is visible a polo necked jumper, c. 1973

*French knickers and brassière,
c. 1975*

*Winter coat in suede or sheepskin
with fur collar and cuffs. The
flared trousers have turn-ups,
c. 1973*

late 1970s full skirted petticoats, from the waist only, were often made of broderie anglaise or had lacey and decorative hems that peeped from beneath the full skirts that were fashionable once again.

Pyjamas as night attire were generally replaced by night-dresses which in the 1960s became so short and transparent that matching panties were worn with them; these were known as Baby Doll pyjamas.

All underwear and nightwear became known as lingerie.

OUTDOOR WEAR

In the early 1950s many coats had very full skirts, achieved either by pleating or by flares. Pockets tended to be large and deep. Many coats were made in reversible materials, usually plain on one side and checked or with some other design on the other. Tweed was a very popular material.

With the straighter skirts, three-quarter length coats or jackets were fashionable; these were generally very flared from the shoulders and had loose fitting sleeves. The coats could be so amply made that they resembled capes. Fitted coats as well as tent style coats with a swing back effect were worn.

High cape collars were popular and some coats even had scarves attached. The length could vary and might be as short as three-quarter length. Fairly straight coats that could have full sleeves tapering towards the wrists were also seen. The collar and cuffs were often of a contrasting or plaid material.

In the 1970s coats were often made of a lighter weight material, such as showerproof gabardine, corduroy, etc. Many had matching hoods or hats.

Duster coats, first worn in the early 1950s, were made reversible and were worn as summer coats or for evening wear. They were generally made of a heavy taffeta silk. Very often they had no fastening but were wrapped around. A belt, when worn, could encircle the coat waist or be threaded through holes in the seam at waist level to draw in the back and allow the front to hang free or vice versa.

From the mid-1950s coats were generally loose fitting and could have shawl collars or large stand-up collars. Straight coats might be without any collar and some coats tapered at the knees or might be three-quarter length. Often half belts were worn low down.

From the early 1960s fur trimmings were used on coats,

jackets, hats, suits. The fur could be real or, more often, of fabric. Immitation or 'fun' furs made of nylon or other man-made materials were made in a variety of colours, not always intended to simulate real fur. They were very popular in the 1960s as they brought glamorous coats within the reach of many. Sheepskin and suede coats also became increasingly popular as the 1960s progressed and were dyed in many colours. There were so many coat styles available that the silhouette varied enormously from short dome-shaped coats to three-quarter-length tapering or flared coats.

In the 1960s collars tended to stand away slightly from the neckline and jackets and coats became less full and straighter with the shoulders rounded. Coats could be loose fitting, either dress or three-quarter length, and the popular sleeves were either dolman or raglan styles worn with large collars. Wrap-over styles with large shawl collars were also worn. About 1962 coats were so amply cut that they gave the appearance of capes.

Towards the end of the 1960s coats became long (what was known as maxi length), almost reaching to the ankles. These coats were worn over mini skirts with knee high boots.

From the early 1960s new weatherproof and water-repellant materials were widely used for raincoats. These new synthetic materials allowed for greater variety of colours and could be used to simulate real leather if wanted. PVC plastic (polyvinyl chloride) which was shiny and could be brightly coloured was much used for jackets, coats, boots and shoes, bags and hats. A 'wet look' using PVC became fashionable. Waterproof nylon was also very popular.

Reversible coats were sometimes made of two different materials, perhaps proofed poplin or gabardine and a woollen fabric. One side was often in the same material as a dress or suit. These coats became very popular as they were ideal for travelling as well as for town wear.

Coats were made in all lengths and the styles varied from straight to flared, with or without belts; the waistline could also be modified according to the dictates of the designers.

From the early mid-1970s capes and caped coats became extremely fashionable because they could be comfortably worn over the popular layered clothing. Capes were made fitted over the shoulders.

In the late 1970s coats made of a type of blanket material

Three-quarter length coat with patch pockets, roll neck jumper and beret style hat, c. 1973

Mohair wrap-over coat with tie belt and a soft hat, c. 1974

Sandals and shoes, c. 1974

and unlined, with large patch pockets, were worn. Also, coats with flared swing backs like those that had been so popular in the 1950s began to return in favour.

FOOTWEAR

In the 1950s England became the centre for shoe fashions, taking the best designs from various countries. Pointed toes originated in Italy while woven uppers on soft and formal shoes came from Spain. America's contribution was the comfortable moccasins with hand lacing; and velvet embroidered sandals came from the East. Spanish, Italian and French shoes were all sold in Britain and their influence was to be seen in many British designs.

T-bar shoes remained in fashion in various guises throughout the century. Clogs were another type of shoe that remained fairly constant throughout, with round dipping toelines and rounded heels or wedges. The uppers might be of strong materials such as gabardine or leather while the soles and heels were of leather, rubber, wood or cork.

Sling-back court shoes were another timeless style, being modernised only by the shape and height of the heels. Plain court shoes formed the basic style for many shoe variations: keeping to the basic shape and just adding decorations such as bows and buckles helped to keep costs down. Very often the decorations could be clipped on so that one pair of court shoes could be used with different embellishments to give the illusion of several pairs of shoes.

The shape of shoes generally were fairly round toed and punched designs were very popular in the 1950s. As skirts became shorter, heels became higher and ankle straps, which had not been so popular in the 1940s, were again fashionable with both high and low heeled shoes. Towards 1955 the toes of shoes became less clumsy in look, and the heels also became more shapely.

In the 1950s casuals as well as elegant shoes all tended to have pointed or elongated toes. The heels, lower for casual shoes, were often made of wood or plastic and covered with real or imitation leather. Patterned or stacked leather effects were often printed on the heel covering or these might be decorated with jewels or studs. Transparent plastic heels with designs on them were also seen for a brief period. Platforms were popular for casual shoes which included sandals and brogues.

When peep-toed shoes and platform soled shoes became

unfashionable, very thin soles with the heels tapered became the mode. The toes were less rounded and gradually became more and more pointed until about 1959 they reached a point a good 4 to 5 cm beyond the natural toe line, thus forcing women to buy shoes as much as two sizes larger than normal. These shoes were known as winkle pickers.

In the early 1960s 'chisel' toes appeared; these toes were squared at the ends, thus shortening the shoes again.

The fashionable A line silhouette in clothes was echoed in shoe styles with pointed toes widening to the vamp. The soft leather used in shoes could be pleated or gathered to help achieve this effect as well as to make decorative patterns.

By about 1962 toe shapes had again altered, this time to become slightly more rounded; although still tapered and slightly elongated they gave a more elegant look than the short rounded toe shapes of the 1940s.

High stiletto heels with narrow pointed toes were popular in the late 1950s but shorter versions also appeared with lower heels. These started broad at the top narrowing right down. These pointed heels were all strengthened with a steel support which was protected by a strong plastic coating under the leather covering. If the outer casing came off, which happened not infrequently, and just the metal tip was left exposed, this made small indentations on floors, lino and carpets as if nails had been hammered in. Stilettos were not popular with some householders and dance floor owners for this reason!

The winkle picker type shoes with stiletto heels were gradually replaced by lower square-heeled and toes shoes that could have ankle straps. The heels remained slender but by about 1967 they again became thicker and the toes more rounded.

The straighter, simpler silhouette of clothes was echoed in the more comfortable and functional shoes that followed winkle pickers and stiletto heels in the late 1960s. Shoes

Various shoes, c. 1978

Unisex plimsoll or running shoes with wedge heel, c. 1977

Men's slip-on shoes, also worn by women, c. 1978

Brogue type shoe, c. 1978

Boot of the late 1970s

Various shoes, c. 1978

*Court type shoe with bow,
c. 1975*

and sandals became wide strapped and chunky heeled with very high platform soles. Shoes with fairly high front tabs which concealed elastic gores beneath were popular for wear with trousers. Waterproof snow boots, usually fastened up the front or side with a zip, were very popular throughout the 1950s. They were usually fur lined, the outside being of suede.

Boots were often made of fur fabric and had hats to match them. Many were just fashion boots and were unlined so that the modish styles would not be too much altered, while those worn for warmth alone were often fleece lined and had rounder toes. They were often made of suede. Smart boots were often high heeled and reached the ankles. They often fastened in the front with either lacing or buckles, although zips were also used. For après-ski, boots were often made of waterproof fabrics that were nevertheless decorative. Wedge heels were general.

Clothes with the leather look which originated with the Mods and Rockers of the mid-1960s made high almost-to-the-knee boots fashionable. Plain casual boots or shoes that fastened with a zip often had large rings or tabs at the end of the zips, with a decorative shape as adornment. The zips themselves were large and chunky and were made in a variety of bright colours. Knee high boots usually had the zip on the inside of the leg or at the back. Boots that reached above the knees were also popular with the mini skirted styles (around 1967) and either fastened with zips or were made of a stretchy material; they usually had rounded toes.

Boots continued in fashion into the 1970s. They could be laced up the front or sides and were often of suede or canvas and trimmed with leather. Shoes became narrower towards the toes and colours more adventurous; a great deal of footwear was made in colourful shiny plastic. Clogs were also worn in all seasons, closed for the winter and open-toed for the warmer weather. Sandals made in leather or fabric

Sandals and shoes, c. 1974

began to have shaped heels. Sandals and canvas shoes for leisure wear could have rope soles which had in fact been in use since the 1950s.

Towards the end of the 1950s thonged sandals made of plastic or leather became very popular as they could be worn in the street or at the seaside; they were flat soled with just two straps from the sides that were joined to the sole at the front between the toes. These were very popular throughout the period until the late 1970s; some even had toe rings and could be quite ornate. Many were in Indian designs and styles and were sometimes known as 'flip flops'.

Hollow heels became a fashion, as were heels with a gap through the wedges for a brief while in the 1960s; this fashion, known as 'doughnuts', returned for summer sandals in 1978.

Shoes with either sling backs or ankle straps sometimes had an elastic gore in the back to give a tighter fit.

Flat ballerina-type shoes were worn for all occasions through the period. Evening shoes were often made of new improved materials and very often sequins were stuck to a fabric upper to form patterns. Lace could also be placed over leather, and transparent plastic for uppers was very popular.

New manufacturing methods such as injection moulding and the ability to weld man-made materials together all helped to alter shoe fashions. New materials also made an impact. Lurex, for instance, came on the market and was used mainly for evening shoes. It was made of untarnish-

Wedge heeled sandal, c. 1976

Strapped shoe, c. 1975

Strapped high stiletto heeled shoe, c. 1975

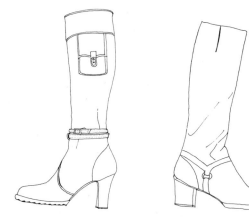

Boots of the late 1970s

Transparent plastic shoe with open toe, c. 1977

Ladies sandals, c. 1978

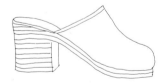

Clogs with various tops and heels, c. 1976

able metallic thread encased in a plastic coating and could be either woven or knitted. Lurex meant that you could wear glittery shoes which could, moreover, be bought to match your evening dress.

Seamless stockings first appeared about 1952 but they were not very popular initially as they laddered easily and were not as well shaped as the fully fashioned ones. Towards the end of the 1950s tinted nylon stockings became popular but it wasn't until the 1960s that stockings and the new tights were available in a wide variety of patterns and colours.

From about 1960 nylon tights as well as stockings without seams made on circular machines were worn, the newly available stretch nylon helping to give them a good fit. Fishnet and patterned tights were much worn with the mini skirts, being much more practical.

Tights could be worn with stretch vinyl boots but also the stretch vinyl high boot look could be achieved by wearing ordinary plain court shoes, low or high heeled, over matching stretch vinyl sockettes which were made to simulate leather; these could reach to any height from calf to thigh.

HEADWEAR

Although so many hat styles were available, the trend set during the War years to go hatless became a habit. Only older women, who had been used to wearing hats before the War, wore them frequently while the younger generation wore hats only for weddings and special occasions; and in the winter to keep the head warm.

Hats were already getting less popular in the 1950s and shops that dealt exclusively in headwear went out of business, leaving the larger department stores to sell the hats still required for certain social occasions. The most popular styles were fairly plain pillbox types that could be decorated with flowers, feathers or tulle to the wearer's taste.

In the early 1950s hats were still worn off the face in all sizes and styles and could be tilted to one side. Smaller hats worn straight on the head made their appearance and could be covered with a veil to the tip of the nose. Head hugging caps, such as small turbans and caps that just covered the crown of the head, were also in the mode. Many were of a stiffened straw or fabric to give a firmer fit. Some hats became so small that they were just small pieces of material profusely trimmed with flowers, ribbons and veiling. Pillbox styles as well as small cloche and beret styles were all worn in the 1950s. Sailor type and coolie hats were also popular.

The small and flat large-brimmed hats continued to be fashionable, but in the early 1950s deeper crowns and more forward angles came into vogue. Flowerpot shapes with small or no brims could be decorated with wide ribbons or tulle.

By the beginning of the 1960s larger brims were again popular. The beret style had gradually became more bouffant and could be made of tulle, chiffon or any lightweight material for summer, being gathered on to a band that fitted around the head. For winter wear it could be made of a fleecy material or fur fabric. Large fur hats were also popular. For summer large net or chiffon toques were sometimes decorated with flowers or bows. In winter fur hats were always in vogue, as were turbans and woolly hats.

Headscarves were worn a great deal both as protection from the cold or rain and to prevent the hair from being blown about in the wind.

Plastic rain hoods, either shaped or made to fold into a small sachet, were extremely useful, either worn over a hat or by themselves, and have remained popular throughout, although hardly fashionable!

In the early 1970s large floppy peaked caps became fashionable; some were known as baker boy caps. Also in the early 1970s, a masculine type of hat made its appearance. This was deep crowned with a wide brim, rather like a stetson or Spanish sombrero, and often had a wide band around the crown with a buckle decoration.

Large straw sun hats which had been popular for genera-

Large brimmed hat, c. 1974

Floppy headscarf-like hat, c. 1963

Pith-type helmet hat with headscarf, c. 1970

Floppy brimmed hat, c. 1972

Peaked cap, c. 1973

Hat with brim turned up in the front, c. 1972

The girl in the red dress is following a 1950s style. The skirt is full, in a peasant fashion, and the bodice has a low décolletage. The matching square scarf is folded diagonally and worn around her shoulders. The sandals also are similar to those worn in the 1950s.

The girl in the tweed trilby hat is wearing a cowl-necked pullover under a zip-fronted sheepskin jacket with patch pockets. The cord trousers fit into calf length, sheepskin lined boots. The young man is wearing a brushed denim suit with a T-shirt. The hat is of the Baker Boy style. The whole outfit is unisex and could be seen just as easily on a girl.

The girl on the right has an ankle length skirt, the matching belt around a long high halter-necked top. This ensemble could be worn for day wear as well as in the evening. (Mid 1970s)

The man is wearing a casual suit, also suitable for formal occasions. It is seen here with an open necked shirt over a high necked pullover.
The young girl in the suede three piece costume has a jacket with wide lapels and patch pockets. The short waistcoat also has wide lapels. The skirt has a slight flare. The shirt blouse is worn open necked. The sandals are of the 1950s style with high platforms and ankle straps. She is carrying a shoulder bag. The girl on the left is wearing a summer frock, the top of which is shirred and has shoulder straps. The skirt is gathered in layers, from beneath which can be seen the edge of the broderie anglaise petticoat. The wedge-heeled espadrille style sandals and basketwork bag are also reminiscent of the 1950s. (1970s)

Hat, c. 1971

Floppy cloche-style hat, c. 1973

tions continued in vogue until the early 1970s when they were worn mainly at weddings, garden parties and race meetings. They were generally decorated with flowers and ribbons.

Caps and berets worn throughout the period are about the only headwear to survive to date, being mainly worn in the winter for warmth. Headsquares or triangular scarves are much more popular than hats as they are practical and offer some protection to the hair.

HAIRSTYLES

Hair rollers were first used in the 1950s and were used to set the hair, allowing it to be lifted with back combing to form a soft frame around the face. A hair lacquer was then used to hold the hair in place.

Very short hair was fashionable throughout the 1950s, the bubble or urchin cut, with soft curls all over the head, being very popular. This style persisted throughout, sometimes with the hair slightly longer.

Older women began to grow their hair longer as hairdressing aids such as tints and lacquers became more widespread while the younger generation wore their hair up to show that they were grown-up. So, in the mid-1950s, hair was very often worn with the front and sides up in a bouffant style while the remainder was allowed to hang down in waves or curls. Highlights were achieved by bleaching streaks of hair. This was popular for both men and women.

In the early 1950s a short hair cut was often left medium length at the nape of the neck as this was found to be more

Beret, c. 1974

Knitted cap, c. 1973

Low brimmed hat, c. 1973

flattering than short hair at the back with off-the-shoulder or strapless dresses.

By the mid-1950s longer and softer, more bouffant hairstyles were introduced. The extra fullness and height was achieved with the use of backcombing. Large rollers employed in setting the hair also helped bring about this effect. By the end of the 1950s these smoother, less curly, hairstyles were well established. Hair was quite often brushed over the forehead.

Around 1950 short hairstyles as well as slightly longer hair worn up at the sides and also up at the back, were seen. In Coronation year, soft fringes and shortish hair combed up at the back were fashionable as this type of hairstyle allowed tiaras and coronets to be worn on top of the head by Royalty and their styles influenced the general public.

Casual looking hairstyles became extremely popular and short fringes were also seen. In the mid-1950s hair was worn straighter with less curls and waves and flatter on the top; it also gradually became slightly longer. Very short hair with the sides turned up and a longer style, more bouffant with the sides puffed out, were fashionable. Fringes were

Hat, c. 1974

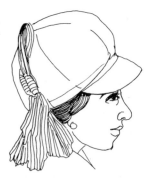

Baker boy floppy cap, c. 1977

Floppy hats, c. 1968

Schoolgirl type hat, c. 1972

Sun hat made in segments, c. 1971

Turban or cloche style hat with sunglasses perched on top, c. 1963

also still popular in the late 1950s, and the bouffant hairstyle was piled high on the head, resembling a beehive. This effect was achieved with backcombing and with the addition of extra hair or top knots. The high bouffant hairstyles hastened the decline in the wearing of hats.

In the 1950s film stars popularised ringlets or curls but towards the 1960s a windswept appearance which allowed for straighter hair, became fashionable. In the early 1960s a page-boy hair cut, sometimes with a small fringe curled under and known as a bang, and with shoulder length hair, also turned under, was quite fashionable.

In the late 1950s wigs, pre-set in a style, became popular, but they were expensive. Later, in the mid-1960s, wigs were not only made of human hair but could be bought cheaply in man-made fibres which were easily washed and dried, being permanently set in a style, either long or short. These wigs could be in any colour; women could thus change the style and colour of their hair as they wished.

Hair pieces could also be bought to match the natural hair to make it appear longer and fuller. Lengths could be bought either curly or plaited and added to real hair so that any style could easily be achieved at home without the aid of experts. Ringlets were sometimes attached to the hair at the back with the hair left flat on the top and waved to the back giving a Victorian appearance.

In the early 1960s wigs became really popular as they facilitated a change of appearance and many people acquired at least one wig or a hair piece.

Hairstyles in the 1960s went to extremes: long straight

Various hat styles, c. 1972

Hairstyles, c. 1975

hair became fashionable for both men and women as did Afro hair cuts. Hairpieces and wigs were still very popular.

By 1960 there was a great variety of hairstyles, mostly with shortish hair, and with all the hair preparations available, most women managed to find a style to suit them.

In the late 1960s hairstyles mainly followed the contour of the head. Chignons were worn with the hair pulled back, leaving the front and sides fairly flat. To add softness a new kind of hairpiece made up of small tendrils or curls, could be attached to the sides giving an old-fashioned appearance.

Hairstyles followed the trendy way of dress and styles became softer and more casual than in previous times. Permanent waves which had in the past been set in tight curls and formal waves were replaced by looser and more informal effects which were achieved by the use of large rollers. These gave the hair a bouffant look, and with the addition of skilful cutting, a natural appearance. Blow drying hair achieved volume and softenss without setting the hair in rollers at all and this custom persisted throughout the period. Colour tints helped older women to camouflage grey hairs so that they were completely unnoticeable.

Three-quarter length hair or reaching just below the ear lobes was one of the most popular lengths and the basic hairstyle popular throughout the period was with the hair combed off the forehead and either a side or centre parting. The hair was allowed to hang down freely in curls, waves

Hairstyles of the 1970s. Some could be wigs or have added hairpieces

or straight. Quite often, especially for special occasions, the top of the hair would be backcombed to give it more body and a raised and full appearance.

In the mid-1960s, when it was fashionable to have long hair, many teenagers wore pony tails. The hair was gathered up and fastened at the crown with either elastic or a band, the loose ends being allowed to fall down in curls. Other ways with long hair included wearing it in a bun or in a French pleat.

Hair partings became unfashionable and the hair was brushed so that the sides flicked up or fell forward just over the cheeks.

Wide elasticated ribbons were fashionable and the hair was often dressed around them. Very often the hair was arranged more to one side, leaving the other side sleek.

Towards the mid-1960s hair became sleeker and was not worn so high on the head. Waves and curls were also fashionable and the styles, both long and short, varied according to taste. From the mid-1960s long straight hair with a centre parting and a fringe was worn, this hairstyle was fashionable with the mini fashions.

For evening wear large chignon pins and leather buckles were worn in the high hairstyles, many of which had the interest focussed on the back.

In the early 1970s for a brief while it was fashionable to have short hair brushed into a crown of short curls on top of the head but as this style suited few women it did not last very long. Hair was mainly to just below ear level with a side or centre parting and waved with hair tongs.

BEAUTY AIDS

Soap which had been rationed during the War was again freely available from the end of 1950. Soapless shampoos which were first introduced in the 1930s remained in use. Many varieties of shampoo were made to suit dry, normal and greasy hair. Hair tints and dyes also came into more general use and were marketed so that they could be used in the home without the expertise of a hairdresser.

Home permanent waving kits were also available and hair lacquers and setting lotions all helped to improve the appearance of hair. With the advent of cold waving methods, softer and more natural hairstyles could be accomplished with the added improved abilities of hairstyling and hair cutting.

Eye make-up became very popular and was manufactured

in many different colours and textures, from creamy to frosty. Powder and cream eye shadows were both available in the 1970s. Eye shadows of compressed powder could be bought in a kind of paintbox while other eye shadows were made like lipstick. Shimmering effects were obtained with eye shadows to which fish scales had been added and these were extremely popular, especially for evening wear. More sophisticated man-made ingredients were later substituted for fish scales.

Eyes were further accentuated by a black or dark brown or blue line along the eyelid, just above the lashes, which might be used to elongate the eyes. These eyeliners could be in pencil form or a liquid paint applied with a small brush. At the height of the fashion for eyeliner, the waif-like look it could be used to give, was reinforced by short, urchin style hair cuts.

Mascara which had previously been obtainable only in block form and applied with a wet brush to the eyelashes, could now be bought in semi-liquid form, contained in pen-like holders which held a 'wand' or narrow circular brush to which the mascara clung and with which it was applied.

Face powders had previously created a pink 'English Rose' complexion for all types of colouring. In the 1950s powders and foundation creams could also be based on yellows and pinks which produced beige or ochre colours that suited darker and more sallow skins, thus glamorising more women.

The darker shades of face powder were also popular because it was fashionable to look suntanned. Sun oils and lotions became increasingly popular as well, as they both protected and helped tan the skin. For those who didn't tan well instant tanning lotions were available; these turned the body the required hue overnight.

With the new range in face powder colours, lipsticks and matching nail varnishes also came in a new variety of colours. The dark and vivid red hues of the 1940s were replaced by paler and more natural shades. These paler coloured lipsticks took the emphasis off the mouth so that more attention was paid to eye make-up.

Pearl effect as well as glitter were available in nail varnishes as well as lipsticks. Nail varnish could also be bought in plain colours with a clear varnish containing the glitter or pearly finish to be painted on at will. In the 1960s it was also possible to buy nail varnishes in almost any colour, even yellow, green, mauve and black. False fingernails and eye-

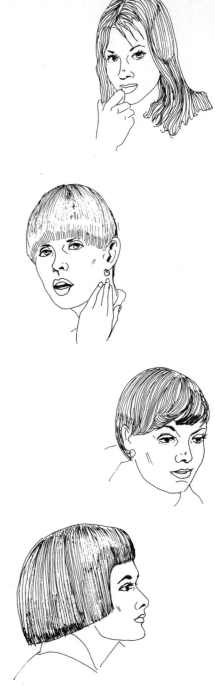

Hairstyles of the 1970s. Some could be wigs or have added hairpieces

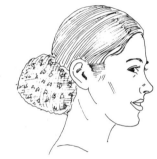

lashes were among the many new beauty aids that were convenient and easy to use without expert knowledge. This led among other things to the decline of the manicurists and make-up artists who had been employed by many hairdressers.

Face masks which were very easy to apply, became available in the late 1950s and hair dyes helped in saving hairdressing costs.

Television and film make-up techniques advanced the use of make-up in emphasising the use of shadow make-up to enhance the bone structure as well as to make the most of the eyes. Fashion magazines for both older and younger women had many articles showing how to make up creatively.

In the late 1970s make-up was used to achieve a less made-up look; the natural look became more studied.

Cosmetic surgery became accepted and many women had their noses altered or ears flattened and had face lifts to remove wrinkles.

ACCESSORIES

In the mid-1950s basket type handbags in a variety of shapes became very popular for summer use. Handbags became larger and were mainly carried over the shoulder as they became similar to flight bags. Handbags in general became bulkier with added front and side pockets. Some had adjustable straps or had two, so that they could be carried over the shoulder or in the hand.

Belts became very popular in the late 1960s with the return of the waistline. They could be made of chain or leather or any type of material and could become very ornate. Even suede or leather belts often had metal chains threaded through or were decorated with metal studs.

Large metal buckles were also fashionable and shoes also sported them on the front, as well as a chain decoration. This mode became fashionable in the late 1960s. Also in the late 1960s, zip fasteners, instead of being just functional, suddenly became an impressive accessory. Used on coats, suits, gloves and bags as well as knitwear, they were made large and chunky in bold colours and often had ornamental tags attached.

In the 1950s plastic or metal covered with fabric, often velvet, hairbands known as Alice bands could be very decorative and might be worn on any occasion. Hair could be draped over them and they were made springy, fitting over the head and ending just behind the ears.

Large rings set with uncut stones began to be fashionable in the 1950s. Large chunky jewellery of all kinds was popular, including glass, plastic and metal pieces. Artificial jewellery became the mode. Large paste and plastic earrings and brooches as well as buckles and clasps were worn. Long rows of beads that could be wound around the neck several times were also fashionable: they could hang down low, almost to the waist, or be short, of the choker kind. Chunky rings and bracelets were also seen. From the mid-1960s much Oriental and Indian style jewellery was in vogue.

Earrings were very popular in the 1950s and 1960s and were made with clips or a screw fastening so that it was not necessary to have the ears pierced. Many earrings were made of light and coloured plastic and could be very large. They were made in the shape of flowers and a great variety of abstract designs. Pendants and long drop earrings were both popular.

In 1978 a new kind of earring fastening came on to the market which made the wearing of earrings more attractive. This used tiny magnets, one placed behind the lobe of the ear and the other, attached to the earring itself, in the front.

Costume jewellery made of glass and metal as well as plastic became so popular that it was and still is worn by all classes, even those who can afford the real thing. Chunky silver rings, bracelets and necklaces became very fashionable from the 1960s and the fashion was to wear a number of rings at the same time. Many new ideas and designs were employed, and enamelling and pebbles, perspex and any other conceivable material were used.

In the 1950s there was a sudden mode for decorative spectacle frames of plastic in a variety of colours inlaid with stones, sequins and glitter dust. The shapes were sometimes quite exotic with the wings at the outer corners vastly exaggerated. Men invariably wore very heavy horn-rimmed spectacles. Sunshades and parasols were replaced by sunglasses from the later 1950s.

Stoles were extremely fashionable throughout. These were long scarves worn for day or evening wear, often in place of a wrap. They were made of mohair, fur, lace, almost any fabric in fact. Many woollen stoles were heavily fringed at the ends. Large triangular or half round scarves, decorated around the edges, were also popular. These were draped over the shoulders and were made for both day and evening wear.

Scarves were very popular as they were so versatile. Long ones could be wrapped around the head to give a turban effect or worn as a belt, and squares and triangles worn over the head and tied beneath the hair at the back. These styles became especially popular in the late 1970s.

Head-hugging knitted caps and cloches with matching scarves became very popular from about 1972.

UNISEX AND CULT CLOTHES

In the 1950s the Beat Generation made its influence felt on fashion. Beatnik girls generally wore black or thick woollen stockings and sandals, loose-fitting polo-necked pullovers and tight figure-clinging skirts and duffle coats. Their hair was usually long and rather untidy and their make-up on the pale side.

In the mid-1960s hippies and 'flower people' started the mode for long kaftans and long dresses with printed designs. They also wore military type clothing bought from second-hand shops. Later their style changed to a more cowboy-type of fashion with fringed leather jackets and moccasins. Beads as well as scarves around the head completed their mode of dress.

Unisex clothes were already beginning to be worn by the early 1950s when matching jerseys and jumpers were made for male and female alike but they didn't really get going until the 1960s.

The back view of unisex styles made it difficult to distinguish between male and female as both wore their hair long, wore similar tops and usually jeans, which became the mainstay for both sexes from the late 1960s.

For winter wear black plastic or leather suits decorated with brass studs were popular while for summer wear hipster jeans and T-shirts were general. In 1966 demin suits were made identical for both male and female, the casual jackets being of a safari type. In the early 1960s the tendency towards unisex clothes allowed women to wear trouser suits more freely; conversely it was the increasingly wide acceptance of women in trousers that led to unisex clothes. In 1965 women's trouser suits, although popular, were not allowed in smart restaurants and hotels but by the 1970s they were accepted in most places.

About 1964 ladies' trousers began to be fastened in the

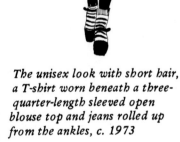

The unisex look with short hair, a T-shirt worn beneath a three-quarter-length sleeved open blouse top and jeans rolled up from the ankles, c. 1973

The girl on the left with matching knitted cap and long scarf is in a knickerbocker-style trouser outfit, short sleeved, under which is worn a high necked pullover, c. 1968. The boy, centre, is a skinhead with hair almost shorn off, and his trousers held up in the popular way with braces. The girl on the right is wearing a mini dress

Jersey top worn with striped shorts, tights and a short jacket. The casual shoes are of the sneaker or running type, c. 1971

The zipped short jacket is worn over a laced-up top and hot pants. The suede boots reach above the knees, c. 1971

front with a zip fly (like men's trousers) instead of at the side and as the 1960s progressed, the front fastening was used more and more.

Unisex clothes in the mid-1960s consisted of Levi trousers or jeans with a front fly zip worn with jumpers, shirts and shirt blouses and cravats or scarves. Sports tops were also popular and flat soft shoes were the usual footwear.

Hot pants, very short shorts, became the rage in 1971. They could be worn under short skirts or slitted minis; worn on their own they could be seen at every type of occasion. Hot pants were made in a variety of materials from satins and silks to denim, cotton, leather or suede. The design varied: they might be cuffed, with pockets, patterned, etc. Short tops showing a bare midriff, tie-dyed T-shirts, halter-necked tops, skinny sweaters and vests were all worn with hot pants as were colourful tights and knee or thigh high boots, or even open laced sandals.

Dungarees, always popular amongst the young, became fashionable in the 1970s. They were made in an assortment of colours and fabrics apart from denim, from velvet to leather. ·

With greater freedom generally clothes became less cumbersome and men did not always have to wear a jacket. However the move towards informality and casual clothes did not mean a lessening in smartness. The advent of synthetic fibres made it easier to keep clothes looking good. It also meant that clothes could be produced more cheaply so that people could keep up with the ever changing fashions.

Men's clothes were tailored for women with the coats narrower at the shoulders, and the jackets longer, to cover the hips. From about 1971 it was fashionable for women to wear smocks over jeans which again gave more of an air of femininity. Shoes were similar, except that women's heels were slightly higher. The unisex theme was stressed by hair salons serving both men and women. Even the hats worn were similar.

Levis or jeans were first worn in the United States, being practical working clothes originally made from tent material by Levi-Strauss in the 1850s. Later, demin dyed blue was used and copper rivets were added for extra strength at the joins. In the 1950s they were made for men only, the students having made them popular, but by the 1960s girls also wore them. They were mainly made in blue denim, other colours having been experimented with, but never becoming popular.

Jeans were worn for durability and convenience but fashion has often taken them a long way from the original working clothes.

Jeans usually had slashed or patch pockets, welted seams and fly fronts. The bottoms were without turn-up and sometimes even left unsewn. They might be tight, flared or bell-bottomed according to fashion. In 1971 it became the craze for jeans to be patched. appliquéd designs, emblems, buttons and embroidery were all sewn over holes or were used just as decoration. Unisex even reached as far as expensive clothes such as Burberry coats where the double-breasted model, for instance, was the same for both men and women except that the buttoning was reversed.

Jeans never lost their popularity, being at their most popular from about 1972. Since they were basically alike in colour and design, the distinguishing feature was the label on them. Details such as studs or even the stitching on the pockets were also of importance. Although jeans were worn by all classes the labels gave them status. The most expensive made by Gucci are cut so as to accentuate the bottom and are made especially long so that they can be wrinkled, but most important, they display the 'G' in studs on the back pocket. At the end of the scale the Punk Rockers wear their jeans loose and baggy with side straps so that the chains, keys and other heavy accessories can easily be attached.

Punk clothes became fashionable in 1977 when Punk Rock music became popular. This was mainly motivated by the high unemployment amongst the young and also by rebellion against society. The fashion was for safety pins to be inserted through the nostrils, cheeks and earlobes. Hair was dyed green, purple, yellow, red or other gaudy colours and was chopped to make it look really unkempt. Make-up consisted of the most bizarre colours — lips painted blue or black and the eyes highlighted with all manner of eye shadows and mascara.

Deliberately torn clothing was held together with safety pins. Punk clothes also included black leather slashed jackets with bicycle chains and razor blades, handcuffs being worn as a decoration. The shabbier the clothes, the more fashionable they were.

This fashion, begun by working class teenagers, soon became commercialised and T-shirts and ripped dresses held together with large safety pins were sold as fashion gimmicks.

Casual shirt top worn with hot pants in a stretch material. The sandals, platform soled, have ankle straps, c. 1971

60

The girls are in pyjama suits. The girl on the left has a sleeveless top, c. 1963, while the one on the right has a sleeveless tunic dress over very wide trousers, c. 1969. The boy in the centre is in a casual unisex belted shirt and jeans, c. 1969

The girl on the left is in a track suit. Track suits were worn by both sexes as well as children. They were of a jersey material with the waistband, wrist and ankles in ribbing for a close fit. The boy in the centre is in shorts and a loose shirt-like top worn over a T-shirt or vest. The small boy is dressed for the sport of skate-boarding with knee and elbow guards as well as a crash helmet, c. 1977

Children

Children's clothes were designed for practicability rather than just being replicas of grown-up clothes. Baby clothes, instead of being constricting, were made so that freedom of movement was possible. Small babies wore all-in-one suits of a material that allowed for stretch and fastened all the way down the front. As they grew up a little romper suits were worn. Toddlers wore mainly pull-on clothes, such as dungarees with a bib in front, with sweaters worn beneath. For summer wear playsuits were popular for all ages. These were similar to dungarees but short legged.

Man-made fibres helped revolutionise children's clothes as they were easily washable and required a minimum of ironing. Little girls wore short dresses with flared or circular skirts while little boys wore shorts and T-shirt type tops.

Synthetics also influenced footwear. Many rubber or synthetic soles and heels, now made in one, had designs stamped on them. These allowed for longer and harder wear and were especially attractive for children's shoes as quite often they were in picture form.

School uniforms became less severe. Girls wore blouses or shirts and ties with skirts in the fashionable length while boys wore shirts and ties and either shorts or trousers as they grew older. V-necked pullovers in the school colours were also worn as well as blazers with the school badge. Caps and school hats were seen less and in the 1970s very few were seen at all.

When the film *Davy Crockett* was first seen, around 1955, American frontier style clothes became very popular. They consisted of soft moccasin shoes worn with jackets and trousers with fringes down the sides as well as Davy Crockett fur hats with a tail hanging down the back.

Young girls who liked their hair long often wore their hair in pony tails, tied up at the back. This style had the hair brushed straight back from the forehead and up from the nape of the neck, and then held on the crown with either a hair ribbon or special clasp, the ends of the hair being allowed to hang down loosely.

The children are wearing the practical clothes of the period

Glossary

Armband	Elasticated or metal band to hold up long sleeves.
Basque	Short skirt-like addition to an upper garment
Battledress Blouse	Blouse with buttoned cuff sleeves, waist length and with attached belt
Beret	Round piece of material gathered to a band to fit the head
Bermudas	Type of shorts reaching the knees
Bikini	Abbreviated bathing costume consisting of a brassière-like top and briefs
Blouson	Belted blouse
Bolero	Very short jacket with or without sleeves, usually collarless
Boutique	Small shop specialising in inexpensive originals and accessories
Bowler Hat	Rounded hat, stiff and with a curled brim
Bow Tie	Small tie, tied in a bow
Bra-slip	Foundation garment with brassière and petticoat in one
Brassière	An uplift undergarment
Briefs	Short knickers
Broderie Anglaise	Open embroidery on white linen or cotton
Brogues	Sturdy low-heeled shoes
Bush Jacket	Similar to a safari jacket and usually made of water repellent material with breast and side pockets, belted and cuffed sleeves
Bustforms	Foam or rubber pads moulded and worn inside a brassière to give a better shape
Cami-knickers	Combined camisole and knickers
Camisole Top	Close-fitting bodice top with shoulder straps
Cap Sleeves	Short sleeves cut in a semi-circle
Car Coat	Short overcoat
Cardigan	Jumper or sweater buttoned or fastened down the centre front

Cheesecloth	Plain woven thin cotton material
Chelsea Boots	Boots with elastic down the sides
Chemise Dress	Dress similar to a shift dress
Chignon	Hair twisted in a knot at the back or nape of the neck
Classical Suit	Usually comprises a fairly plain straight skirt and matching single- or double-breasted jacket with collar and lapels
Cloche	Small hat with tiny brim, coming low over the head
Clogs	Type of shoes raised off the ground with wooden, leather or cork soles
Court Shoe	Plain shoe without any front fastening
Cravat	Neckcloth or tie
Crew Neck	Flat round neckline
Cross Pocket	Horizontally sloping pocket
Culotte	Type of divided skirt
Cummerbund	Wide waist sash
D.A. Hairstyle	Hair brushed back from the sides, meeting at the back
Décolletage	Low neckline
Denims	See *Jeans*
Dinner Jacket	Jacket like a lounge jacket
Dirndl	Skirt, fully gathered at the waist
Dolman Sleeve	Sleeve like a raglan, but with a deeper armhole, almost to the waist
Double-breasted	Closure with a double row of buttons overlapping
Drape	Wide shouldered jacket
Dungarees	Trouser and bib-topped overalls
Duster Coat	Loose flared lightweight unlined summer coat
Empire Line	Dress silhouette, belted or tight to beneath the bosom and then hung loose chemise-like
Fair Isle	Colourful bands of geometric design on knitwear
Flares	Gradually spreading out of material
Fob Watch	Small pocket watch
Gauntlet Gloves	Gloves with long extensions beyond the wrists
Godet or Gore	Triangular piece inserted for extra width or flare
Hairpiece	False piece of hair
Halter Neck	The front of a garment fairly high leaving the shoulders and back bare
Hipsters	Trousers or jeans cut as high as the hips and held up with a belt
Hot Pants	Very short shorts
Inverted Pleats	Box pleats in reverse, folded in pairs
Jabot	Frilled front of shirt or blouse
Jeans	Strong cotton trousers, usually of denim reinforced at the joins with copper rivets
Kaftan	Long coat-like Oriental long-sleeved garment

Knife Pleats	Single creases pointing in one direction
Lapel	Folded back part of front of jacket or coat
Layered Look	Many items of clothing worn one on top of the other
Leotard	Body stocking of stretch nylon with long or short sleeves. The leg part could also be very brief
Lounge Coat	Shortish jacket without a seam at the waist
Mandarin Collar	Short standing collar attached to a close fitting garment
Maxi	Long skirt almost reaching the ankles
Midi	Skirt reaching below the knees to mid calf
Mini	Skirt well above the knees
Moccasin	Slip-on shoe of very soft leather
Morning Coat	Coat similar to a tailcoat without cut-away fronts, just sloping towards the back
New Look	Style designed by Christian Dior in 1947; small waisted bouffant skirts to calf length
Panti-girdle	Foundation garment, pants made of elasticated material, combination of knickers and corset, sometimes with attached suspenders
Patch Pocket	Pocket sewn on to a garment
Peep-toe Shoes	Type of court shoe with the front toepiece cut out
Pencil Skirt	Straight close-fitting skirt
Petticoat	Underskirt
Pillbox Hat	Small round hat
Pinafore Dress	Sleeveless dress usually worn over a blouse or jumper
Platform Shoes	Shoes with thick soles raising them off the ground
Pleats	Series of folds
Plimsolls	Canvas shoes usually with rubber soles
Polo Neck	Round necked pullover
Pullover	Jumper put on over the head without any fastening
Punk	Rubbishy or worthless clothes held together with safety pins
Pyjamas	Loose trousers and top for nightwear
Quiff	Lock of hair on the forehead
Raglan Sleeve	Seam reaching from underarm to neckline
Rever	Turned-back edge of a garment revealing the under surface
Roll Collar	Collar without points, also known as a shawl collar
Roll Neck	High-necked round opening folded down
Sack Dress	Straight hanging dress
Safari Style	Hunting type outfit in cotton, usually with patch pockets and matching belt
Sandal	Straps or cut out uppers attached to a sole
Set-in Sleeves	Tailored sleeves sewn to fit into an armhole
Shawl Collar	Collar without points
Sheath Dress	Tube-like straight dress
Shift Dress	Shortish dress, usually smocked or gathered at the shoulders

Shirtwaister	Dress, usually buttoned to the waist or all the way down, either with or without a belt. Usually with a small collar
Shorts	Short above-the-knee type of trousers
Single-breasted	Closure with a single row of buttons and buttonholes
Slacks	Sporty or casual trousers
Slip-on	Shoe without any fastening
Stiletto Heels	Very thin steel, covered heels with tiny tips
Suspenders	Loops and buttons to hold up stockings
Sweater	Knitted or crocheted jumper or pullover
T-Bar Shoe	Shoe with a strap along the instep, joining the ankle strap at right angles
T-Shirt	Sports shirt, usually in cotton, with a crew or V neck, with or without sleeves
Tabard	Sleeveless jacket without collar, usually fastened at the sides and worn over jumpers or blouses
Tailcoat	Coat with long skirts at the back joined at the waistline with cut-away fronts
Tent Coat	Coat flared widely from a low collar, giving a tent or A silhouette
Tie-Dye	Hand process of dying, tying off sections of the material to resist the dye
Tights	Skin-tight garment, stockings made in one with briefs
Toque	Small round brimless hat
Trapeze Line	Slight flare at the side seams, A line silhouette
Trench Coat	Coat usually of gabardine or waterproof material with raglan sleeves and with a belt
Trilby	Soft felt hat of Tyrolean shape
Trouser Suit	Tailored trousers and jacket for women
Tunic Dress	Dress slightly shorter than the fashionable length, worn over a skirt or trousers
Turban	Draped band or scarf worn around the head; could be made in a hat design
Turn-ups	Base of trousers turned up
Twin Set	Jumper and matching cardigan, knitted or crocheted
Tyrolean Hat	Wide-brimmed felt hat, usually with a feather in the side of the hatband
Unisex	Similar clothes worn by males and females alike
Vents	Vertical slits
Vest	Originally an undergarment, but no longer so
Waistcoat	Short sleeveless jacket
Winkle Pickers	Long pointed toe shoes

Select Bibliography

Amphlett, Hilda, *Hats*, Richard Sadler 1974

Asser, Joyce, *Historic Hairdressing*, Pitman 1966

Boucher, F., *20,000 Years of Fashion*, Abrams

Bradfield, N., *Historical Costumes of England*, Harrap 1972

Brogden, J., *Fashion Design*, Studio Vista 1971

Brooke, Iris, *Footwear*, Pitman 1972; *History of English Costume*, Methuen 1972

Carter, Ernestine, *Twentieth-century Fashion*, Eyre Methuen 1975

Contini, M., *Fashion from Ancient Egypt to the Present Day*, Hamlyn 1967; *Fashion*,
  Crescent 1965

Cooke, P.C., *English Costume*, Gallery Press 1968

Courtais, G.de, *Women's Headdress and Hairstyles*, Batsford 1971

Cunningham, P., *Costume*, A & C Black 1969

De Anfrasio, Charles & Roger, *History of Hair*, Bonanza 1970

Dorner, Jane, *Fashion*, Octopus 1974; *Fashions in the Forties and Fifties*, Ian Allan 1975

Garland, Madge, *History of Fashion*, Orbis 1975; *Fashion*, Penguin 1962

Gunn, Fenja, *The Artificial Face*, David & Charles 1973

Hansen, H., *Costume Cavalcade*, Methuen 1956

Harrison, Molly, *Hairstyles and Hairdressing*, Ward Lock 1968

Hartnell, Norman, *Silver and Gold*, Evans 1958

Howell, Georgina, *In Vogue*, Allen Lane 1975

Konig, R., *The Restless Image*, George Allen & Unwin 1973

Langner, L., *The Importance of Wearing Clothes*, Constable 1959

Laver, James, *Concise History of Costume*, Thames & Hudson 1963; *Costume*, Cassell 1963

Monsarrat, Ann, *And the Bride Wore*, Gentry Books 1973

Moore, D., *Fashion Through Fashion Plates*, 1771-1970, Ward Lock 1971

Peacock, J., *Fashion Sketchbook 1920-1960*, Thames & Hudson 1977

Pistolese & Horstig, *History of Fashions*, Wiley 1970

Saint-Laurent, Cecil, *History of Ladies' Underwear*, Michael Joseph 1968

Schofield, Angela, *Clothes in History*, Wayland 1974

Selbie, R., *Anatomy of Costume*, Mills & Boon 1977
Streatfield, Noel, *Shoes,* Franklin Watts 1971
Taylor, J., *It's a Small, Medium and Outsize World,* Hugh Evelyn 1966
Wilcox, R.T., *Dictionary of Costume,* Batsford 1970
Wilson, E., *History of Shoe Fashions,* Pitman 1969
Yarwood, D., *English Costume from the Second Century BC to the Present Day,* Batsford
  1975; *Outline of English Costume*, Batsford 1967
Pictorial Encyclopedia of Fashion, Hamlyn 1968

Index

'A' line   25, 30, 38, 44
Accessories   5, 23, 25, 55, 60
Afternoon wear   32, 39
After-shave lotion   8
Amies, Hardy   6, 7
Anorak   14
Ashley, Laura   25, 28

Bag   24, 25, 42, 55; shoulder   23
Balenciaga, Chrisobal   30, 31
Bathing costume   13
Beachwear   38
Beads   56, 57
Beatnik   16, 23, 57
Beatles   16
Beard   22
Beauty aids   23, 53
Bell bottoms   13
Belt   14, 19, 23, 25, 30, 32, 36, 42, 55, 57; buckled   23; cartridge 28; half   14, 25, 41; medalion 23
Beret   23, 48, 49; Basque   7
Bermuda pants   34, 38
Biba   28
Bikini   25, 37
Blazer   63
Blouse   13, 28, 31, 32, 34, 36, 39, 59, 63; battledress   13; Cossack 36; shirt   32, 59
Blouson   34
Bolero   36, 28
Boots   7, 16, 18, 20, 42, 45, 47; bovver   18; Chelsea   20; chukka 16; crêpe soled   16; fashion   45; football   13; high   13, 20, 28, 42, 59; snow   45
Bow   28, 31, 39, 43
Bracelet   56
Braces   18
Bra slip   40
Brassière   27, 40
Briefs   27, 40
Brooch   56
Buckle   19, 22, 43, 45, 48, 53, 55, 56
Bustforms   40
Button   9, 12, 16, 28, 60

Cap   19, 36, 47, 48, 49, 57, 63, baker boy   48; peaked   7
Cape   36, 42
Cardin, Pierre   6
Cardigan   14, 32, 36, 37
Carnaby Street   18
Casual wear   6, 12, 14, 20, 21, 31
Chanel, Gabrielle   31
Chignon   52; pins   53
Clasp   56
Cloche   10
Clogs   45
Coat   7, 11, 19, 25, 32, 38, 41, 42, 55; British warm   7; caped   42;

car   19; casual   6; double-breast- ed   19; duffle   57; duster   41; granny   32; leather   14; motoring 7; over   13, 19; rain   19, 42; reversible   42, sheepskin   38, 42; single-breasted   19; sports   7; sweater   36; tent   6; trench   7, 36
Collar   7, 11, 12, 16, 18; 19, 24, 25, 32, 41, 42; studs   24; high   11; jacket   12; mandarin   7; pinned 7; pointed   12; roll   11; shawl 18, 41, 42; shirt   12, 24; stand-up 41; stepped   16; tabbed   7; velvet   7, 19
Coronet   50
Corselet   40
Corset   39
Courrèges   6
Cravat   59
Crew neck   14, 37
Cuff   9, 16, 18, 19, 41, 59
Culottes   34
Cult clothes   57
Cummerbund   18

Daywear   34, 56, 57
Denim   8
Deodorant   8, 23
Dior, Christian   30
Drainpipes   16
Drapes   16
Dress   7, 25, 30, 31, 36, 37, 38, 50, 57, 63; afternoon   31; chemise 7, 30, 31; day   28; evening 30, 39, 47; gymslip   6, 25; pinafore   13, 25; sack   30, 31; sheath   28, 30; shift   25, 28, 31; shirt   39; shirtwaister   31, 32; sleeveless   28, 31; tennis   38; tunic   30, 31, 34, 36; two-piece 31; wedding   39
Dungarees   59, 63

Earrings   56
Edwardian styles   7, 12, 14, 16, 21, 28
Empire line   30
Ensemble   36, 37
Epaulettes   7
Evening wear   18, 27, 32, 34, 37, 39, 41, 53, 56, 57
Eye, liner   54; mascara   54, 60; shadow   54

Face mask   55
Fair Isle   37
False, eyelashes   54; fingernails   54
Flower people   18, 57
Footwear   20, 43, 59, 63
Formal wear   11, 13, 18, 39

Girdle   40
Gloves   24, 25, 55
Gucci   60

'H' line   30
Hair   16, 21, 22, 39, 50, 51, 52, 53, 55, 57, 60, 64; band   55; dye 55; laquer   43, 53; lights   49; piece   21, 51; rollers   49; salon   59, spray   22, 23; tongs 53
Hairstyles   7, 16, 21, 22, 23, 49, 50, 51 52, 53; crew cut   21; D.A.   21
Handbag   55
Handkerchief   11
Hat   7, 19, 23, 25, 38, 39, 41, 42, 47, 48, 59; beach   13; beret 47; bowler   11, 16, 23; cloche 47; coolie   48; Cossack   23; felt   19; fur   48; pillbox   47; sailor   48; school   63; straw 48; trilby   23; Tyrollean   23
Headscarf   38, 48, 49
Headwear   19, 23, 39, 47
Hell's Angels   16
Hippies   18, 22, 57
Hipsters   7, 13; jeans   14
Hood   41; rain   48
Hot pants   6, 25, 28, 59

Informal evening wear   9
Informal wear   13, 28, 31
Ivy League   16

Jabot   11, 19
Jacket   7, 9, 11, 12, 13, 14, 16, 19, 25, 28, 30, 31, 32, 34, 36, 37, 41, 42, 57, 59; bush   13; cardigan 14; casual   14, 19; Chinese   7; corduroy   14; dinner   7; double-breasted   9, 14, 18; gabardine   14; leather   16; padded   14; single-breasted   14, 16, 18; sports   7, 9, 13; sweater 14
Jeans   5, 8, 13, 14, 16, 20, 32, 34, 38, 57, 60; hipsters   57; Levi   59
Jerkin   32
Jewellery   56; costume   56
Jumper   7, 25, 32, 37, 39, 57; hooded   32; polo neck   7

Kaftan   7, 36, 39, 57
Kimono   7, 37
Knickers   40; cami   40; Directoire 40; French   40
Knitted material   12, 14
Knitwear   7, 55

Lapel   9, 11, 14, 18
Layered look   14
Leisure wear   13, 31, 37

Leotard 32
Lingerie 41
Lipstick 54
Lotion 23; after-shave 23; setting 53; sun tan 23, 54

Make-up 8, 53, 54, 55, 60
Maxi 6, 25, 27, 34, 36, 42
Midi 6, 28, 36
Mini 6, 25, 27, 28, 34, 36, 39, 40, 42, 45, 47, 59; pants 13
Mix and match 11
Mods 16, 45
Morning coat 18
Moustache 22
Muffler 36

Nail varnish 54
Neckerchief 12
Necklace 56
Neckwear 12
Neo-Edwardian 14
New Look 28, 30
Night attire 24, 35, 41

Outdoor wear 19, 41
Over-waistcoat 36

Pantie girdle 40
Panties 40, 41
Parasol 56
Pendant 56
Perfume 6
Permanent waves 52, 53
Petticoat 31, 34, 36, 39, 40, 41; slip 32
Playsuit 38, 63
Plimsolls 20
Pocket 9, 11, 13, 24, 41, 59, 60; breast 18; cross 13; flaps 9; hip 28; patch 14, 19, 28, 60; ticket 18; vertical 32
Polo neck 14, 37, 57
Poncho 36
Princess line 30
Pullover 13, 14, 28, 36, 37, 57, 63
Punk 5, 60
Pyjamas 24, 35, 41; baby doll 41

Quant, Mary 6, 25, 28, 34

Revers 19
Ring 56
Rockers 16, 45
Romper suit 63

'S' line 30
Safety pins 60
Sandals 20, 36, 43, 45, 46, 57, 59; flip-flops 46
St. Laurent, Yves 6, 30
Scarf 12, 14, 24, 36, 41, 49, 56, 57, 59
School uniform 63
Separates 14, 31
Shampoo 53
Shawl 36
Shirt 7, 11, 13, 14, 18, 19, 24, 36, 63; casual 12, 13, 14; check 11, 13, 38; cheesecloth 36; day 19; evening 12, 18, 19; floral print 12; frilled front 11, 19; Indian 12; leisure 7; open neck 13, 14, 16; polo neck 11; printed 7; sports 7; striped 7, 11; T-shirt 12, 14, 32, 36, 57, 59, 60, 63
Shoes 9, 7, 13, 16, 20, 21, 25, 42, 43, 44, 45, 55, 59, 63, 64; brogue 43; canvass 13, 20, 21, 46; co-respondent 20; court 43, 47; crêpe soled 7, 20; evening 46; moccasin 20, 43, 57, 64, running 20; slip-ons 20; sneakers 20; sports 20; stiletto 41; T-bar 43; training 20; winkle pickers 7, 16, 20, 41
Shorts 11, 13, 28, 32, 38, 63; football 13
Sideburns 16, 22
Skinhead 18
Skirt 6, 13, 25, 28, 30, 31, 32, 34, 36, 37, 40, 41, 43, 57, 59, 63; bouffant 34; dirndl 7, 32, 34; divided 34; evening 32; pencil 34; tennis 38
Slack 11, 13, 14, 34
Sleeves 9, 11, 31, 32, 37, 41, 42; cap 28, 31; Dolman 28, 30, 42; draped 32; raglan 14, 19, 28, 32, 37, 42,; set-in 14, 19, 25, 37
Smock 59
Sockettes 47
Socks 13, 21, 23
Space Age 6
Sports wear 13, 37
Stockings 39, 40, 47, 57; nylon 47; seamless 47
Stole 39, 56
Suit 7, 9, 11, 14, 18, 19, 25, 31, 42, 55, 57; classic 25, 31; denim 14, 57; evening 18; leisure 14;

lounge 9, 18; safari 14, 57; single-breasted 9; trouser 6, 13, 27, 31, 34, 36, 39, 57; velvet 16; Zoot 7
Sun, shade 56; glasses 56
Suspender 40; belt 39
Sweater 14, 25, 27, 32, 34, 36, 59, 63; Arran 14, 32
Swimming costume 37, 38

Tabbard 32
Tailcoat 18
Teddy Boy 5, 7, 16, 20, 21; Girl 25
Tennis outfit 13, 38
Tiara 50
Tie 7, 12, 14, 19, 63; bow 19; bootlace 16; knitted 11
Tights 6, 25, 27, 32, 34, 40, 47, 59
Tops 28, 31, 32, 34, 37, 39, 57, 63; camisole 32; tunic 36
Toque 48
Trapeze line 30
Trousers 7, 9, 11, 12, 13, 16, 18, 20, 27, 30, 32, 34, 35, 36, 37, 38, 45, 64; corduroy 16; Levi 59; tennis 13
Turban 47, 48
Turtle neck 14
Turn-ups 12, 16, 34, 60
Twiggy 27
Twin set 7, 37
Two piece outfits 14

Undergarment 32
Underskirt 34
Unisex 34, 37, 57, 59, 60
Undervest 13, 32
Underwear 27, 39, 40, 41

V-neck 37
Veil 47
Vents, back 9, 16; side 9, 32
Vest 32, 36, 59; sleeveless 36

Waistcoat 7, 11, 16, 32, 36
Waspies 40
Watch, fob 11
Wet look 42
Wig 51

'Y' line 30

Zip 12, 16, 19, 34, 45, 55, 59